T0116789

Becoming Emily

The Life of Emily Dickinson

Krystyna Poray Goddu

CHICAGO
REVIEW
PRESS

Copyright © 2019 by Krystyna Poray Goddu
All rights reserved
First hardcover edition published in 2019
First paperback edition published in 2022
Published by Chicago Review Press Incorporated
814 North Franklin Street
Chicago, Illinois 60610
ISBN 978-1-64160-597-7

The Library of Congress has cataloged the hardcover edition as follows:

Names: Goddu, Krystyna Poray, author.
Title: Becoming Emily : the life of Emily Dickinson / Krystyna Poray Goddu.
Description: Chicago, Illinois : Chicago Review Press Incorporated, [2019] |
    Includes bibliographical references and index.
Identifiers: LCCN 2018024637 (print) | LCCN 2018033675 (ebook) | ISBN
    9780914091004 (adobe pdf) | ISBN 9780914091196 (epub) | ISBN
    9780914091127
    (kindle) | ISBN 9780897330039 | ISBN 9780897330039 (cloth)
Subjects: LCSH: Dickinson, Emily, 1830–1886. | Women poets, American—
    19th century—Biography.
Classification: LCC PS1541.Z5 (ebook) | LCC PS1541.Z5 G63 2019 (print) |
    DDC 811/.4—dc23
LC record available at https://lccn.loc.gov/2018024637

Cover design: Lindsey Cleworth
Cover illustration: Giselle Potter
Interior design: Sarah Olson

Excerpts from Emily Dickinson's poems and letters from the following
volumes are used by permission of Harvard University Press:

The Poems of Emily Dickinson: Reading Edition, edited by Ralph W. Franklin,
Cambridge, MA: Belknap Press of Harvard University Press, Copyright ©
1998, 1999 by the President and Fellows of Harvard College. Copyright © 1951,
1955 by the President and Fellows of Harvard College. Copyright © renewed
1979, 1983 by the President and Fellows of Harvard College. Copyright ©
1914, 1918, 1919, 1924, 1929, 1930, 1932, 1935, 1937, 1942 by Martha Dickinson
Bianchi. Copyright © 1952, 1957, 1958, 1963, 1965 by Mary L. Hampson.

The Letters of Emily Dickinson, edited by Thomas H. Johnson, Associate Editor,
Theodora Ward, Cambridge, MA: Belknap Press of Harvard University Press,
Copyright © 1958 by the President and Fellows of Harvard College. Copyright
© renewed 1986 by the President and Fellows of Harvard College. Copyright
© 1914, 1924, 1932, 1942 by Martha Dickinson Bianchi. Copyright © 1952 by
Alfred Leete Hampson. Copyright © 1960 by Mary L. Hampson.

Printed in the United States of America

This book is dedicated to the memory of
Leslie Maria Farrell Layman (1987–2017)

Much loved, much missed

CONTENTS

Author's Note

In writing about Emily Dickinson, I have often chosen to let the poet speak for herself. This book is filled with quotations from her writings. Author of nearly 1,800 poems and more than 1,000 letters (many of which read like poems themselves), Emily had her own distinctive style. She did not adhere to traditional spelling or punctuation rules. She also wrote different drafts of many of her poems, often changing words and punctuation. She was not interested in publication and so only about 10 poems were published during her lifetime, all of them anonymously and all but one without her permission.

After her death, those who edited and published her handwritten work in print form had to make difficult decisions about which draft of a poem would have been Emily's final choice. They also had to decide whether to keep or change her often-unusual spelling and punctuation. As a result, Emily's work has been published with many variations.

In this book I have used the versions of her poems and letters as presented in the two most widely respected collections. Her poems have been copied from *The Poems of Emily Dickinson: Reading Edition*, edited by R. W. Franklin and first published by the Belknap Press of Harvard University Press in 1998. For her letters, I have relied on the three-volume edition of *The Letters of Emily Dickinson* edited by Thomas H. Johnson with associate editor Theodora Ward and first published by the Belknap Press in 1958. In writing about the Master letters, I have used the reordering done by R. W. Franklin in *The Master Letters*, published by Amherst College Press in 1986. (I am grateful to Dickinson scholar Marta Werner for pointing me to Franklin's 1986 work.)

I'd also like to note the usage of first names for most of the figures in Emily's life. In Emily's time, people—even close friends, sometimes—addressed each other very formally. Many of the important people in Emily's life, such as Thomas Wentworth Higginson, Samuel Bowles, and Otis Phillips Lord, were older men. In spite of feeling very close to them, she never used their first names when writing to them. Often her letters simply begin: "Dear friend." After much thought, I decided to use first names for all the major figures in this book, regardless of how Emily might have addressed them. I hope that the use of first names will help convey the closeness Emily felt to these dear friends, who were so deeply intertwined in her heart and mind.

EARLY CHILDHOOD AT THE HOMESTEAD

Imagine a young woman, small like a wren, with chestnut-colored hair and matching eyes, strolling through a garden ablaze with colorful flowers: yellow heliotrope, pink and purple sweet peas, red cinnamon roses, and white jasmine. These are her children; she lovingly tends to them, year after year. A bobolink sings overhead. Soon she may wander with her big brown dog, Carlo, into the nearby woods, where her favorite wildflowers grow: violets, anemones, pink and yellow lady's slippers, and Indian pipes. She is whispering what sounds like a prayer, but is a poem:

> Some keep the Sabbath going to Church -
> I keep it, staying at Home -

With a Bobolink for a Chorister -
And an Orchard, for a Dome -

Some keep the Sabbath in Surplice -
I, just wear my Wings -
And instead of tolling the Bell, for Church,
Our little Sexton - sings.

God preaches, a noted Clergyman -
And the sermon is never long,
So instead of getting to Heaven, at last -
I'm going, all along.

It is a warm Sunday in June in the town of Amherst, in western Massachusetts. The young woman's family is at church, but she is where she feels closest to God, in nature. Soon her beloved parents and siblings will return, and they will all be together in the home she holds so dear. But for now, Emily Dickinson is blessedly alone in her own sacred place: her garden.

Silhouette of Emily
at 14 years old.

Emily was born in the house that stands near that garden. Built by her grandfather, Samuel Dickinson, in 1813, it was the first brick house in town. When Emily was born there, on the cold Friday morning of December 10, 1830, just before 5:00 AM, Amherst had already been home to the Dickinsons for many generations.

Emily's ancestors had come to western Massachusetts from England in 1659 and had been among the town's founders 100 years later. The Dickinsons, like many English families in the 1600s, had left England because they wanted to simplify, or purify, the Church of England. They called themselves Puritans. Puritans thought the focus in church should be on reading the Bible, listening to sermons, and praying, in ordinary language, not the Latin of the Church of England. They believed that all decorations should be removed from churches and that no music should be played during services. They believed church leaders should be ordinary people who wore ordinary clothes, not priests. They tried to live simple lives of faith in God, hard work, and strict rules. The leaders of the Church of England opposed the Puritan tenets and outlawed them. As a result, many Puritans left England for the new land of America so they could practice their faith freely. By the time Emily was born, Puritanism as a formal religion had died out, but her family, like numerous others in New England, still lived by many of their ancestors' rules and beliefs.

Emily's grandparents, Samuel and Lucretia, lived in the house they called the Homestead, on Amherst's

Main Street, along with several of their nine children, even after the children grew up. Emily was welcomed into the large household by her parents, Edward and Emily, and her brother, Austin, several months shy of his second birthday. She was walking by the time she was 11 months old, and soon after her second birthday she had a little sister, Lavinia, who was called Vinnie.

The Homestead was a big house, set on higher ground than the street, with views of the town center to the west, the surrounding mountains to the east, and a large meadow across the road. When Emily was young, there were ten rooms, but with so many people—sometimes as many as 13—living there, Edward's family had only two bedrooms. Emily, Austin, and Vinnie shared one, and their parents used the other. Edward, a lawyer with a growing political career, was often away on business, and their mother was a shy, quiet woman who rarely showed affection, so the siblings looked to each other for companionship and comfort. They remained deeply close all their lives; they always depended on each other and hated to be separated.

After Vinnie's birth in February 1833, their mother remained weak for several months. When spring came, her sister, after whom the new baby had been named, offered to help by taking two-year-old Emily to her home in the town of Monson, about 20 miles away from Amherst. The journey took a long time in those days and grew frightening when a severe thunderstorm erupted about halfway through the trip. They were in the middle of a pine forest, and aunt and niece were both scared. Emily called the lightning "the fire" and asked to go home to her mother. But Aunt Lavinia managed to protect the little girl from much of the rain by covering her with her cloak. They made it to Monson that night.

Aunt Lavinia found little Emily to be "a very good child." She took her to church, where she behaved well, and to visit her maternal grandparents, who were pleasantly amused by her. She sewed a gingham apron for her niece to wear. And, according to Aunt Lavinia, Emily enjoyed her long visit very much; she "is perfectly well and contented," Lavinia wrote to her sister, adding that Emily had learned to play the piano—"she calls it the *moosic*"—and other than talking sometimes about big brother Austin, she "does not moan for any of you."

Perhaps Emily was content because she had older cousins for playmates at the house in Monson—William, who was 10, and another Emily, who was 4. They were the children of her Uncle Hiram, her mother and Aunt Lavinia's brother who had recently died of consumption (a disease of the lungs now known as tuberculosis), and his widow, Amanda, who was now suffering from the disease. Besides caring for her young nieces and nephew, Aunt Lavinia was busy nursing her sister-in-law, Amanda, during Emily's visit.

Not yet three years old, Emily lived in the atmosphere of illness and death that filled the house. While she most likely didn't understand exactly what had happened to her late uncle, or why Aunt Lavinia sometimes seemed sad and worried, she would surely have absorbed the anxiety and grief that surrounded her.

The visit lasted about a month, and when it was time for Emily to return to Amherst, Aunt Lavinia found herself lonely without her sweet companion. Emily had left behind the gingham apron, and when Aunt Lavinia found it, she wanted to cry.

Soon after Emily's return, her grandparents left Amherst. Their departure was felt keenly not only by Edward's family—Emily and Austin had lived with their grandparents for all of their short lives—but also by the entire town. Samuel had been a prominent though not wealthy member of Amherst society. He had served his community as a landowner, lawyer, and political representative. A firm believer in educating girls as well as boys (a radical view in that time), he had helped found Amherst Academy, a coeducational school, in 1814. He went on to help establish Amherst College, which opened in 1821.

But his zeal for these institutions was expensive. He had given so much money to the college that by 1833 he had run out of funds and had to sell the Homestead. He was offered a job in Cincinnati, Ohio, and moved there with Lucretia and their two youngest daughters. Emily never saw her grandfather again. Edward rented half of the Homestead from the new owners, the Macks, so his family—including his youngest brother, Frederick—could continue to live there.

It was from the Homestead, then, that four-and-a-half-year-old Emily—with big brother Austin as her protective companion—left for her first day of school in September 1835. The primary school was a two-story whitewashed brick building, about half a mile from the Homestead. The education provided was far from stimulating. Over the five years Emily attended the school, she learned only the basics: reading, writing, and simple arithmetic.

When the weather was cold or stormy, or the ground deep with mud, as it often could be in western

An 1845 silhouette of the Dickinson family; from left: mother Emily, Vinnie, Austin, Emily, and father Edward.

Massachusetts, her parents kept Emily home. If it was terribly bad, they kept Austin home, too. But he was a boy, stronger and older, so they were more worried about Emily's health than his. And even though the Dickinsons believed firmly in education for girls, in Edward's mind, Austin's education was more important than his sister's. Away on one of his frequent business trips, Edward wrote to his older daughter, "You must not go to school, when it is cold, or bad going—You must be very careful, & not get sick."

In the mid-1800s, illness was frightening, especially when it hit children. Many of the Dickinsons' friends and relatives had lost their children to diseases that began with a simple cough or a rash. Fearful, Edward liked to order his family to bedrest at the slightest sign of sickness. If any of them grew ill while he was away, he rushed home.

Her father's concern meant that Emily spent nearly as much time learning at home as at school. When she was seven years old, her father advised her in a letter to "keep school, & not disturb Mother" and to "learn, so as to tell me, when I come home, how many new things you have learned since I came away."

"Keeping school" meant doing her lessons at home. She was to learn things by memorization so she could recite them upon his return. And although Emily wasn't supposed to disturb her, her mother sometimes sat with her and oversaw her schoolwork, especially the written parts.

Emily's father, Edward
Dickinson.

Edward also regularly
admonished the chil-
dren not to cause their
mother any trouble or
anxiety. He worried a lot
about his wife, who was
not only shy and quiet
but also often nervous. She
was a hardworking, frugal
housekeeper, preferring not to
pay for a servant but to do all the
housework herself. The house was always spotless. She
was an excellent cook and a devoted gardener. She grew
roses and figs—especially difficult in that climate—that
were the talk of the town.

As in many New England households in the mid-
1800s, father ruled in the Dickinson home. When
Edward was home, he began every day by reading the
Bible to the family. Then he led them in prayer. The children were expected to obey their parents without question. In a letter Edward wrote them while on another
business trip, he expressed how happy their good behavior made him: "My Dear little Children, Your mother
writes me that you have been quite good since I came
away.—You don't know what a pleasure it is for me to

have such good news from you—I want to have you do perfectly right—always be kind & pleasant, & always tell the truth, & never deceive."

Years later, Emily may have been remembering how constricted she felt by the expectation to always be well behaved when she wrote a poem that began like this: "They shut me up in Prose - / As when a little Girl / They put me in the Closet - / Because they liked me 'still' - ."

It's doubtful that she was literally shut up in a closet. But sometimes she felt that her naturally playful and lively spirit had to be locked away.

At age 21, though, she remembered in letters to friends how much she had enjoyed the freedoms of childhood. To one she wrote that she yearned to "ramble away as children, among the woods and fields, and forget these many years and these sorrowing cares, and each become a child

Emily's mother, also named Emily.

again." When she was 22, she wrote to Austin that she wished they could do the "things we did when children," adding, "I wish we were children now."

Things she liked to do included the squishy joy of wading in the mud. Once she lost one of her shoes in the mud and arrived home barefoot. Her mother didn't scold or punish her as she usually did when Emily was too loud or misbehaved. This time, Emily remembered, her mother merely "frowned with a smile"—probably because Emily had also been looking for flowers as she waded.

She, along with Austin and Vinnie, loved to read. There weren't many books or magazines published for children in the 1830s, but when Emily was six, Edward arranged for them to receive the *Sabbath School Visitor* every month. Meant to inspire young readers to love and fear God and to lead a good and moral life, it was edited by Emily's uncle, Asa Bullard. Every month the *Sabbath School Visitor* included a (probably fictional) story about the harrowing death of an innocent God-loving child. There was Frederick, who fell into a barrel of boiling water at the age of three and, just before dying, turned over his last 60 cents to religious missionaries. Another month, devout Abigail died of an enlarged heart. Two issues were devoted to four-year-old Charles, who went blind and then died a painful death, all without a word of complaint.

Happily, Edward's next magazine subscription for his children was a little lighter in tone. When Emily was seven, the monthly *Parley's Magazine* began to arrive in the Dickinson home. Also published for children, each issue of *Parley's* offered material on travel, biography, history, poetry, moral tales, and puzzles, including rhymed riddles or other brainteasers.

Although Emily was an avid reader at a young age, she was not inspired to write poetry or anything else during her childhood. Until she was nine years old, her life centered around the Homestead, playing with her siblings, pleasing her father, and not worrying her mother. The religion she took for granted in her very youngest years began to seem increasingly mysterious: the Bible verses she heard in church, the hymns the congregation sang, the daily readings her father presented to the family, the stories in the *Sabbath School Visitor*—all made a strong impression on thoughtful Emily.

A Beloved School
with Beloved Friends

When Emily was nine, her father decided it was time for his family to have an entire house to themselves. His law practice was doing well; the Dickinsons did not have to worry about money. In the spring of 1840 he bought a large home on West Street, not far from the Homestead. It sat on more than two acres of land bordering Amherst's cemetery, which could be seen from the rear windows on the second floor. There was room for a garden, an orchard, and grapevines, and Austin even planted a small grove of pine trees.

The children often walked with their mother in the nearby woods, looking for wildflowers and other natural treasures. They discovered yellow lady's slippers, white Indian pipes, pink-and-white trillium, and climbing fern. As she grew older, Emily became known for her gardening skills, but wildflowers—especially small ones—were always her favorites. By the time she was a teenager, there was hardly one she couldn't identify.

Early in 1840 a traveling portrait painter, Otis A. Bullard (no relation to Emily's uncle Asa), arrived in Amherst. Edward liked the idea of having permanent

The Amherst home where the Dickinsons lived from 1840 to 1855.

This portrait of the three Dickinson children—from left: Emily, Austin, and Vinnie—was painted in 1840.

images of his family. He hired Bullard to paint indi-vidual portraits of himself and his wife and one of their three children together. For the sitting, Austin, Emily, and Vinnie put on their good clothes—a black white-collared suit for Austin and white-lace-trimmed dresses for the girls (dark green for Emily, silvery-blue for Vinnie). The painter gave Emily an open book with a rose laid on its pages to hold.

That autumn, Emily and Vinnie enrolled at Amherst Academy, which Austin was already attending. A three-story brick building, it was an enormous leap from the school Emily had attended for the previous five years. She loved her seven years at Amherst Academy. The remarkable school, which had begun accepting girls only two years earlier, had an open-minded curriculum that included a strong emphasis on the sciences. The level of studies was exceptional. Students were even allowed to attend science lectures at nearby Amherst College. The teachers were young and passionate. Many of them had just graduated from the college. Friendships between students and teachers were encouraged.

Emily was one of about 100 female students. It was at Amherst Academy that she first began to be recognized for her original and inventive writing. A teacher later described her as "very bright, but rather delicate and frail looking." He called her an excellent scholar, whose compositions "in both thought and style seemed beyond her years, and always attracted much attention in the school and, I am afraid, excited not a little envy." One older classmate recalled that Emily and another girl were "the wits of the school." Another one remembered Emily often surrounded by girls at recess, listening with fascination to the funny, peculiar stories she was making up on the spot.

Amherst Academy.

Emily's schoolmates were able to admire her writing because Amherst Academy held regular essay competitions. Every other Wednesday the entire student body gathered in a large hall on the third floor to listen to each other recite their original compositions. (A sign of the school's progressive thinking was that girls were encouraged to express themselves through reciting their words aloud. In that time, women were generally discouraged from public speaking.)

Some of the girls also occasionally produced a publication they called "Forest Leaves." The pages were passed around the school, and each student who wanted to contribute wrote her piece in script. Emily's small, precise handwriting was always recognizable.

Emily's classes included Latin, which she studied for at least three years. Even though she and her good friend Abby Wood scribbled notes to each other in the Latin textbook they shared, the poetry she later wrote shows that she learned the ancient language well. She also studied history, algebra, geometry, and several sciences, including botany and geology.

Amherst Academy was so well regarded that families from distant towns often sent their daughters there. The girls would board with Amherst families while attending school. One of these girls, Jane Humphrey from Southwick, 35 miles away, lived with the Dickinsons for a few months. Jane was a year older than Emily, and the two grew close. On spring afternoons, when the school day was done, they sat together in the Dickinsons' front doorway and listened to the birds chirping in the cherry trees and a farmer chopping down a tree in the nearby woods. Sometimes the rustle of one of their dresses frightened the birds away. At night they jumped, giggling, into the bed they shared.

In the spring of 1842, the close Dickinson family life was interrupted by Edward's decision to send Austin, just 13 years old, away to school. The newly formed Williston Seminary in Easthampton already had a reputation as an even more demanding school than Amherst Academy. It was less than 15 miles away from Amherst, but any distance seemed too far to Emily and her siblings; it was the first time since Emily's visit with Aunt Lavinia that they had been separated. Emily missed Austin terribly from the start.

One of the first letters she ever wrote was to Austin, only a few weeks after his departure. "You cannot think how odd it seems without you there was always such a Hurrah wherever you was," she lamented. In between sharing news about the hens and their egg-laying and neighborhood affairs, she pleaded, "you must write oftener to us." Other than numerous marks—like periods in midair—separating some of her thoughts, her letter includes no punctuation.

The days were quieter without Austin, but life went on. Emily counted the eggs the hens produced daily and worried about Austin's favorite rooster. Their other two roosters liked to gang up on him, and she worried that they would eventually kill him. It didn't help her spirits that spring always came late to western Massachusetts. Not until the first days of May could Emily write Austin that the trees were finally full of blossoms.

As if it weren't bad enough that Austin was gone, Jane had left Amherst, too. Although she had other friends, Emily missed Jane. She wrote not only to her brother but to her friend as well, entertaining Jane with local gossip. One of their friends had received a gold ring from a boy they knew. Emily's plants were growing beautifully. The other roosters had finally succeeded in killing Austin's favorite.

In the letter to Jane, Emily's blossoming wit comes through in her description of a classmate reciting his composition about the importance of thinking twice before speaking. Emily concluded that "he is the sillyest creature that ever lived I think. I told him that I thought he had better think twice before he spoke." But the stories and jokes are framed by her longing for her friend: "I miss you more and more every day, in my study in play at home indeed every where I miss my beloved Jane—." The letter to Jane was the first of many Emily would write to her friends throughout her life, expressing intense emotions for them while cleverly weaving in anecdotes, descriptions, and deep reflections.

In spite of missing Jane and Austin, Emily continued to thrive at school and in her community. The school day at Amherst Academy began and ended with prayer. Students were expected to attend church on Sunday as well as Bible class on Saturday evenings. Emily's family were prominent members of Amherst's First Congregationalist Church. For 12 years, week after week, Emily sat in the Dickinson family pew, listening to the young minister, Rev. Aaron Merrick Colton, preach and pray in bold, musical, but unadorned tones. When she began to write poems, they bore the evidence of Colton's stylistic influence.

In late April 1844, when Emily was 13, her second cousin Sophia Holland, who was two and a half years older and a close friend, grew ill with typhus, a very dangerous infectious disease. Emily was terribly distressed by Sophia's illness and spent as much time as she could by her bedside. She later described their closeness by saying "my thoughts & her own were the same."

As Sophia grew worse, she became delirious. Now Emily was forbidden to go into her room. She felt as though she herself would die if she couldn't see Sophia. Not until it was clear that Sophia was dying was Emily allowed to say goodbye to her friend. She took off her shoes and silently entered the room. She described the experience a few years later in a letter: "There she lay mild & beautiful as in health & her pale features lit up with an unearthly—smile. I looked as long as friends would permit & when they told me I must look no longer I let them lead me away. I shed no tear, for my heart was too full to weep, but after she was laid in her coffin . . . I gave way to a fixed melancholy."

While Emily didn't talk about her grief at losing Sophia, she fell into a depression that was obvious to her family and worried them. Her parents decided to send her to visit Aunt Lavinia, who was now married with a small daughter and living in Boston. The month with Aunt Lavinia and her two-year-old cousin Louisa— Emily called her Loo—helped lift her spirits.

On the way home from Boston, Emily stopped for a few days in Worcester with her uncle William, her father's brother. At Uncle William's she received another lift to her spirits when a letter from her father arrived. He wrote, "Tell Uncle Wm. that I want a Piano when he can buy good ones, at a fair price." Emily had long been wishing for a piano. Even though it would be nearly a year before a piano arrived in the Dickinson household, the prospect of it made her very happy.

Emily returned to Amherst on a Wednesday in early June, just in time for the essay recitations at school. She had missed the final weeks of the spring term and the first two weeks of the summer session. During her absence, a new girl had enrolled at Amherst Academy. Emily first saw her on the staircase going up to the third floor. She noticed her immediately because the girl wore dandelions in her hair. Emily was intrigued.

She quickly befriended the girl, who was Abiah Root from Feeding Hills, a small village near Springfield, about 25 miles south of Amherst. Abiah was staying with cousins while attending Amherst Academy. She was, to Emily's fascination, working on a novel. She and Emily formed a close circle of friends with three other girls. Emily called them "the five."

The fall term at school was a joyful one for Emily. Not only did she revel in her friendships with the five, but she and her friends also adored their teacher, Elizabeth Adams, who had come from Syracuse, New York, the previous December. Sunday evenings Emily went to singing school. Austin had returned to Williston Seminary, but her friends and her beloved teacher made his absence a little easier to bear. By spring, however, the circle of five began to fall apart.

SCIENCE, NATURE, AND RELIGION

Abiah Root was the first of the five to leave Amherst. By early 1845 she was back in Springfield, attending Mary B. Campbell's school for girls. She gave Emily a lock of her hair as a remembrance, and Emily treasured it. The two kept up their friendship through letters, Emily's full of gossipy news about friends and family. She was eager to read Abiah's novel, she wrote, and was still going to singing school Sunday evenings.

Late February brought unusually mild weather to Amherst, and Emily rejoiced that her plants thrived. By now her mother had taught her a great deal about gardening, and it was becoming one of her greatest passions. She wrote to Abiah that "it seems more like smiling May crowned with flowers than cold, arctic February, wading through snowdrifts. . . . My plants look beautifully. Old King Frost has not had the pleasure of snatching any of them in his cold embrace as yet, and I hope will not." Whether she realized it or not, Emily was already using literary devices, such as describing frost as a person, to add life to her writing.

Years later she would write a poem about fighting back against the oncoming cold weather that continued this personification. The first two verses read:

> The Frost of Death was on the Pane -
> "Secure your Flower" said he.
> Like Sailors fighting with a Leak
> We fought Mortality -
>
> Our passive Flower we held to Sea -
> To mountain - to the Sun -
> Yet even on his Scarlet shelf
> To crawl the Frost begun -

Emily's great love of plants and flowers was enhanced by her botany studies at Amherst Academy. Her textbook, *Familiar Lectures on Botany*, was written by Almira Hart Lincoln in 1829 and was very popular in schools. From this book Emily learned the structure and patterns of different kinds of plants and their Latin names. Lincoln wanted her readers to understand her belief that the beauties of nature reflect the workings of God. She criticized those who "admire the gifts, while they forget the giver." She dedicated her book to the Divine Purpose, as God was often referred to in those times.

Lincoln's approach to the study of botany as a reflection of God's goodness was echoed in most of the subjects being taught at that time. Science and religion (namely, Christianity) were not seen as conflicting; rather science was seen as proof of religion. Studying the sciences was considered a way of learning and better understanding God's creations.

This belief in the important relationship between science and religion was also the foundation of the geology lectures Emily attended at Amherst College that year. Presented by the college's president, the well-known scientist Edward Hitchcock, the lectures inspired the entire Amherst community and probably greatly influenced Emily's intellectual development. Like Lincoln's botany textbook, Hitchcock's lectures focused on accurate scientific knowledge of the natural world as a way of appreciating the magnificence of the God who created it, according to religious teachings. Other girls her age in New England may have been attending finishing schools to perfect their needlepoint and dancing, but Emily was learning the chemistry behind the colorful autumn foliage.

Learning science was not limited to the classroom or lecture hall. Emily also took part in nature walks on which students identified plants and flowers, pointing out their specific characteristics. On these walks, students gathered specimens, which they dried, pressed, and labeled in blank books they called herbariums. Emily began her herbarium that spring of 1845. Over time she would collect and preserve more than 400 plants and flowers in it.

Many of Emily's poems are filled with references to plants and flowers. When she wrote, "I pull a flower from the woods - / A monster with a glass / Computes the stamens in a breath - / And has her in a 'Class'!" she was referring to the system of classification that she was taught in botany lessons.

One day in early May, when Vinnie had gone to Boston for a two-week trip with their father, Emily went out alone to pick wildflowers and marvel at the beautiful spring trees covered with fragrant blossoms. Later that day she wrote Abiah about her herbarium, enclosing a geranium leaf as encouragement for Abiah to create her own. "'Most all the girls are making ones," she told Abiah. "It would be such a treasure to you." She offered to send Abiah some local Amherst flowers.

Two girls of the five were still at school with Emily—she and Abby Wood worked together at a table. By now, though, another had left Amherst to attend school in Pittsfield. Dear Miss Adams was gone, too. Emily missed her two good friends and her teacher very much.

Emily continued to excel in her writing and jokingly bragged about it to Abiah: "I have written one composition this term, and I need not assure you it was exceedingly edifying to myself as well as everybody else." Now 14 years old, she was also growing interested in her own

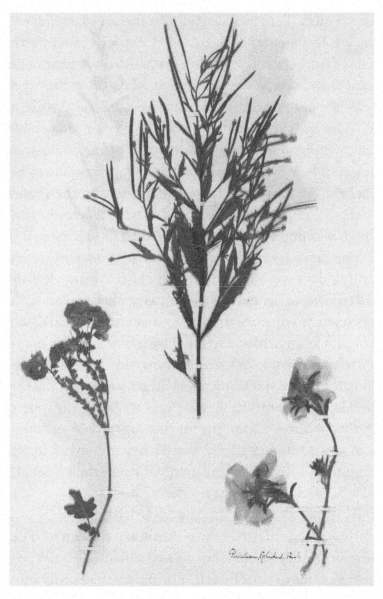

An original page from Emily's herbarium: she labeled only one of the specimens on this page.

appearance. "I am growing handsome very fast indeed!" she wrote flippantly to Abiah. "I expect I shall be the belle of Amherst when I reach my 17th year. I don't doubt that I shall have perfect crowds of admirers at that age."

When summer came, Emily, who was now wearing her hair up, the mark of a young woman, finally had her own piano and was delighted to be taking lessons. Her aunt Selby was staying with the family and was her teacher. They used an instruction book by the French classical composer, pianist, and teacher Henri Bertini, which was popular at the time. (Abiah used it as well.)

The school summer term was 16 weeks long, and Emily's days were crowded with classes, music lessons, and tending to her garden as well as her house plants. She was trying to squeeze in time to make a bookmark—the design was an arrow encircled by a wreath—for one of her school friends, but it was going slowly. She did find time, though, to pick and press forget-me-nots for all her friends. She promised to send one to Abiah. In spite of Emily's worries about the upcoming school examination, she wrote her friend that "I never enjoyed myself more than I have this summer," praising their "delightful school" and "pleasant teachers."

By now only two of the five friends—Abby and Emily—were still attending Amherst Academy. They were both kept home from school during the fall term, however, due to poor health. The frailty that Emily often experienced as a child continued into her teenage years, often accompanied by a very bad cough. The summer had flown by for her. "I really think someone must have oiled his [time's] chariot wheels," she wrote, "for I don't recollect of hearing him pass, and I am sure I should if something had not prevented his chariot wheels from creaking as usual." (Again, she refers to time as a person, making easy use of this literary device to add interest to her observation.) Even with Abby to keep her company, her illness put her in a downcast mood. Not until a long, affectionate letter from Abiah arrived did the mood lift.

However revived Emily may have felt, her parents did not think she was well enough to return to school. She was allowed to continue her piano lessons, though, and in late September her mother decided it was time to teach her eldest daughter to make bread. Her mother relied on the recipes in a book Edward had given her when they married: Lydia M. Child's *The Frugal Housewife*. One of the standards was Child's recipe for what was called Rye and Indian Bread. Rolling up her sleeves, plunging her hands into the cornmeal, rye, yeast, and water, Emily was delighted with the two loaves that she produced. Bread—and later, desserts—became her specialty.

Late September in western Massachusetts meant the beginning of cold weather, and Emily feared, as always, for her flowers. She had had an especially beautiful garden this past summer, but the flowers were nearly gone by the end of the month. Again, she wrote to Abiah about her enemy, the biting winter chill many people referred to as Jack Frost. "I mean to pick the prettiest ones before I go to bed, and cheat Jack Frost of so many of *the treasures* he calculates to rob to-night." She wished she could send Abiah a bouquet for Abiah to press and poetically label as "the last flowers of summer."

By December Jack Frost had definitely won the battle of the flowers, but a lot of Emily's time was taken up by the large number of indoor plants she cared for. She also practiced piano for two hours a day and continued to take lessons. While her parents didn't think she was strong enough to return to school, they did allow her to attend German classes, which were taught by the principal of Amherst Academy, Stephen Coleman. (His daughters Eliza and the older Olivia were friends of Emily's.) It was unusual to have a course in German in Amherst, and Edward thought this might be Emily's only chance to study the language.

On Christmas Eve, Emily hung up her stocking on the bedpost, as usual. Protestant New Englanders in the mid-1800s didn't consider Christmas a very important holiday; they had begun to observe it with any degree of celebration only 100 years earlier. In fact, Emily's Puritan ancestors had been banned from even recognizing December 25 as a holiday, and the only Christmas tradition the Dickinsons observed was stockings for the children. When Emily woke up Christmas morning, she was pleased to find that her stocking held, among other things, perfume, a sheet of music, pin cushions, needlebooks, and lots of candy.

The start of the new year made Emily gloomy for some reason she couldn't understand. She hadn't heard from any of her three departed friends for too long and missed them. Even though new girls her age had come to Amherst that winter and Emily befriended them, she would have rather had her three old friends "back than all the new comers," she wrote Abiah. She and Abby were still keeping each other company, as neither was yet allowed to return to school.

When Abiah wrote back, her letter was more serious than Emily's. She confided that she had been having deep inner struggles about religion. While going to church, praying, and reading the Bible were a part of daily life for most New England families, it was generally believed that in order to become a full member of the church, one had to publicly proclaim one's belief in Christ. Abiah had recently been considering making such a pronouncement. But did she truly feel she could give her heart to Christ?

Abiah Root, one of Emily's earliest correspondents, about 1847.

Emily delayed writing back, not wanting to influence Abiah's decision. She showed the letter to Abby, and the two pored over it. When Emily did respond to Abiah, she mused at length about her own struggles with the same question: "I feel that I shall never be happy without I love Christ. . . . There is an aching void in my heart which I am convinced the world never can fill." She wrote about death and eternity and about her wish that she could give herself over, but "Evil voices lisp in my ear—There is yet time enough."

She described a local revival of the previous winter, in which people of all ages had crowded church meetings and made their proclamations about accepting Christ. Intrigued as she was, she couldn't bring herself to attend. She didn't trust herself not to get swept up in the excitement. She was afraid she might speak out before she had wholeheartedly made her decision. But she scolded herself for this reluctance: "How ungrateful I am to live along day by day upon Christs bounty and still be in a state of enmity to him & his cause."

Less than two months later, Abiah had made her decision for Christ. When Emily read her letter, she cried and wished that she could have the same certainty. Another of the five friends had also made that decision. Distraught, Emily sat down at her little writing desk and again poured out her yearnings to Abiah. She felt that she had once, briefly, experienced the personal love of God, and the memory of those sweet moments tortured her: "I think of the perfect happiness I experienced while

I felt I was an heir of heaven as of a delightful dream, out of which the Evil one bid me wake & again return to the world & its pleasures." She stopped praying and attending her prayer circle. Friends tried to convince her to return, but she felt her heart had grown too hard and distant from God to do so.

It is hard to fully understand the depths of struggle that Emily must have had with her inner self. She wrote to Abiah with such passion about loving God and wanting to serve him, and yet she could not betray the tiny deep part of herself that resisted this joy. At 15, Emily was developing her singular character; the insistence to live in her own complete truth was becoming her hallmark.

HIGHER EDUCATION

I n the spring of 1846, Emily and Abby were waiting eagerly for a promised visit from Abiah. They planned that she would share her time between their two homes. When their friend, Abiah's cousin, traveled to the small town of Feeding Hills, where Abiah lived, they warned the girl not to return to Amherst without Abiah. When she returned alone—with no explanation except that Abiah could not come—Emily and Abby would barely speak to her.

A bright note was the return of Miss Adams, who was again teaching at Amherst Academy. In the summer, both Abby and Emily were deemed well enough to return to school, and the presence of Miss Adams was a wonderful surprise.

Emily's health began to worsen throughout the summer, but with Miss Adams back, she couldn't bear to stay away from school. After 11 weeks, though, her cough had grown so bad and her throat so sore that she was overcome by weakness and had to stay home. She roamed the fields, picking flowers, but most of her usual duties were limited. The illness brought with it some depression. Late in August her parents decided she might do better if she were away from home for a while. She was sent, as she had been a few years earlier, to Aunt Lavinia in Boston.

The four weeks Emily stayed with Aunt Lavinia and her family were filled with activity. She toured historical sites such as Bunker Hill, where one of the great battles of the American Revolution had been fought, and delighted in the plantings at Mount Auburn Cemetery, which had been founded just after her birth.

In spite of the unseasonable heat, she climbed to the top of the State House. She attended concerts and a horticultural exhibition. She was especially struck by the Chinese Museum, where a Chinese music professor and a Chinese writing master demonstrated their talents (the musician sang, accompanying himself on two instruments) and was thrilled to purchase—for 12½ cents each—two cards from the writing master. One bore her name in Chinese calligraphy. Vinnie's name was on the other.

The visit worked its magic, as her parents had hoped. She returned to Amherst in the middle of September, healthy and in good spirits. Vinnie had taken good care of Emily's garden in her absence. Austin was now enrolled as a freshman at Amherst College. The fall term at Amherst Academy had already started, so it was decided that Emily would not go back until the winter term—which would begin just after Thanksgiving. She kept busy practicing piano, sewing, and generally helping her mother with household affairs. She missed school, especially Miss Adams, and couldn't wait to be back.

Her return to school was bittersweet; this would be her last year at Amherst Academy. Her parents had decided that in the autumn of 1847 she would go away to school, to Mount Holyoke Female Seminary in the town of South Hadley, nine miles south of Amherst. (The school's name changed in 1893 to Mount Holyoke College, and today it remains a highly respected women's college.) It would be a momentous change for Emily: she would live away from her family for the first time in her life. But she was full of excited anticipation and worried only that her health might keep her from attending the new school.

Letters from Abiah continued to remind Emily to reflect upon her relationship with God. Emily gently expressed her doubts to her friend: "I feel that I have not yet made my peace with God. I am still a stranger - to the delightful emotions which fill your heart."

Soon after Emily's 16th birthday in December, Amherst welcomed another traveling artist. William C.

North called himself a "Daguerrian Artist." Daguerreotypes—the first photographs—had been invented in 1839, in France. A sharp and accurate image on a heavy metal plate, a daguerreotype was expensive to create. Emily and her mother each sat for their portraits for Mr. North during his three-month stay in Amherst.

Besides the painting of the three Dickinson children in 1840, this daguerreotype is the only existing image of Emily. She looks directly and somewhat solemnly into the camera, but the beginnings of a smile seem to play on her face. While both Austin and Vinnie were photographed in later years, we must rely on verbal descriptions to imagine what Emily looked like as she grew older.

In her final year at Amherst Academy, Emily was studying algebra, ecclesiastical history (the history of the church),

This daguerreotype taken in about 1846–47 is the only authenticated photograph of Emily.

and the work of the Greek philosopher and mathematician Euclid. She thoroughly enjoyed her last months at the school. Even though Miss Adams had left again—this time for good, as she was to be married soon—there was a new teacher whom Emily loved, Miss Woodbridge. She described her to Abiah in great detail, noting "a most witching pair of blue eyes . . . teeth like pearls - dimples which come and go like the ripples in yonder merry little brook." Miss Woodbridge was affectionate and lovely, Emily declared, and then admitted that she was always in love with her teachers.

Emily's last day at Amherst Academy was August 10, 1847. That summer Abiah finally made her promised visit to Amherst, and the girls delighted in each other's company. On September 30 Emily left home for Mount Holyoke Female Seminary.

The decision to send Emily to Mount Holyoke illustrates the importance the Dickinson family placed on education for girls. In the mid-1800s not many girls went on to higher education. Many families, wealthy and poor alike, believed that marriage was the primary goal for girls, so there was no need for them to be as well educated as boys. Higher education for a boy could be the means to a lucrative profession, which most families hoped their daughters would never need to consider.

That so many of Emily's friends also went on to attend female seminaries reflects the intellectual and privileged circle in which she lived. The Dickinson home, with its strong affiliation with Amherst College, was always filled with educated people engaged in thoughtful political and intellectual discussions.

Female seminaries were not actually colleges but institutions meant to educate girls to the same standard as boys. Three years was usually the length of time it took to complete the course of study. Girls who completed the entire course often went on to become teachers. Many girls, however, stayed only one or two years. Only unmarried women could be teachers, so girls who expected to marry soon felt no need to complete the entire three years.

Founded in 1837 by Mary Lyon, the school had 235 students when Emily was enrolled there. There were three classes—Junior, Middle, and Senior—and upon arrival the students took exams to determine which

This four-story brick building housed both teachers and students at Mount Holyoke Female Seminary when Emily attended the school.

class they would join. (Very few female seminaries required students to take entrance exams.) Emily was worried about the exams. She knew that if she didn't finish them in time she would be sent home. It didn't help that she arrived at Mount Holyoke with a cold, which sapped much of her energy.

She was allowed to put off the exams for a day until she felt better. Then she sat over them for three days and was quite relieved to learn that she had qualified for the Junior Class.

Once she was a member of the Junior Class, Emily's goal was to do well enough to pass quickly into the Middle Class. The courses—and even the textbooks— were similar enough to what she had studied at Amherst Academy that after about six weeks of studies she was promoted.

During the first days of school, Miss Lyon addressed her students on the topic of religion. Just as at Amherst Academy (which Miss Lyon herself had attended as a girl, studying under Edward Hitchcock), all the studies were founded in a belief in God and the Bible. Deeply religious, Miss Lyon was concerned that all the girls in her care find their way to fear and honor God. Her concern was expressed in regular sermons that gently but persistently questioned and encouraged the girls toward proclaiming their faith and belief.

She asked the girls to rise by class, and then questioned each of them as to their faith. Those who did proclaim, or profess, their faith she named "professors" and "saved." Then there were those who seemed to have a hope of being saved. Miss Lyon defined this group as being "with hope." The third group were girls whose responses marked them, Miss Lyon believed, as having no hope of being saved. Early in the year, the third group was a large one. But over the course of the year, as Miss Lyon presented her quiet yet strong sermons, more and more girls found themselves with hope or even saved. To the end of her days at Mount Holyoke, though, Emily remained one of the few in the group with no hope—in Miss Lyon's eyes.

In Emily's own eyes, though, she was full of hope, and that hope was rewarded with each of nature's seasons. Every autumn as she watched the blooms fall off her plants and the trees grow bare, she had not only hope but also faith. She knew without a doubt that, come spring, those plants would flower again and the trees would grow abundant with greenery. The death of the natural world and its rebirth, every year without fail, was all the proof Emily needed of God. She didn't need to profess her faith with words; she experienced her faith through nature.

The Mount Holyoke students and their 12 teachers lived in a four-story brick building, where they ate their meals and attended classes and religious meetings. Miss Lyon did not believe in hiring domestic help. The girls and teachers did all the cooking and cleaning. Emily's job was to carry in the knives for each meal and to wash and dry them each evening.

The days followed a strict schedule. Emily rose at 6:00 AM. Breakfast was at 7:00. From 8:00 to 9:00 she studied. At 9:00 the entire school met in the Seminary Hall for what was called "Devotions"—a time for religious practice. This was followed by ancient history and other studies until noon, when she practiced calisthenics—physical exercise. The midday meal was at 12:30 and was followed by singing and piano practice. At 3:45 the girls all gathered in small groups to account for their behavior during the day. They had to report whether they had been absent or late, broken silent study hours, received company in their rooms, or broken the rules in any other way.

At 4:30 Miss Lyon addressed the students—usually about God and religion. Supper was at 6:00 PM. The evening was devoted to silent study until the retiring bell rang at 8:45, followed by a tardy bell at 9:45—the one the girls absolutely had to obey.

As always, Emily delighted in her teachers. She wrote to Abiah that "Miss. Lyon & all the teachers, seem to consult our comfort & happiness in everything they do & you know that is pleasant." She was happy to be studying botany again, which included roaming in the woods with the other students, searching for plant specimens. Some of the girls had brought their own plants to Mount Holyoke, but Emily had not. She had considered bringing them, but once she got there she was happy that she had left them in Amherst. The school building was cold, and Emily realized her dear plants might not have survived the conditions.

In spite of enjoying so much about her new school, Emily was terribly homesick. It helped that her roommate was her older cousin Emily Norcross, with whom she had played as a toddler, on that first visit to Aunt Lavinia soon after Vinnie's birth. Cousin Emily was in the Senior Class and did her best to keep the younger Emily in good spirits. But it was a visit from Austin, accompanied by Vinnie and Abby, after Emily had been away about three weeks, that truly made her happy. They came laden with gifts—cake, gingerbread, pie, peaches, apples, chestnuts, and grapes. Vinnie brought her a lovely ribbon.

A few weeks later, on a Wednesday afternoon, Emily was sitting by the window when, to her delighted astonishment, she saw her parents walking toward Mount Holyoke. She sprang from her chair, clapping her hands, and did a little dance. Then she rushed downstairs to meet them. They had planned to surprise her and succeeded wonderfully! It was nearly unbearable to let them go at the end of their visit, but she contented herself with the thought that in two and a half weeks she would be going home for Thanksgiving.

The Wednesday before Thanksgiving, Emily awoke to a stormy morning. Some of the girls had left school earlier, so there weren't many at the breakfast table. After the meal, those who remained waited anxiously to be picked up. It seemed like the longest morning of her life, but finally Emily saw the family carriage approaching. She dashed out so quickly she nearly frightened Austin, who had come for her and Cousin Emily.

Soon the threesome was on their way to Amherst in the torrential rain. The wind howled around them, and the brooks they passed were filled with rushing water that threatened to overflow. But Emily couldn't have been happier; she was on her way home for this wonderful holiday.

As she saw the spires of Amherst approaching, Emily's heart filled with gratitude for her safe return home. The rest of her family—including the cat—met her at the door. Emily was moved to see tears in her mother's eyes. The storm raged all night, but Thanksgiving dawned bright with dazzling sunshine.

Unlike Christmas (when many schools did not even close), Thanksgiving was an important New England holiday. The Dickinsons celebrated it like other New England families. The day began at church, where Emily enjoyed Reverend Colton's excellent sermon. The family returned for a splendid Thanksgiving dinner at noon, relishing the traditional turkey and mince pies and reminiscing about past holidays.

The afternoon saw numerous visitors; the Dickinsons themselves had four separate invitations for the evening. Emily regretted that they could accept only two. They spent an hour with the family of an Amherst professor, and then the young people—Emily, Austin, Vinnie, and Cousin Emily—met up with a group of friends at one of their homes. They played games until the clock pealed 10. When they returned to the Dickinson home, Edward was still up and in the mood for piano music. So

Emily finished her eventful holiday by playing several songs for him.

The next few days were equally filled with friends and family. When Monday came, Emily reluctantly returned to Mount Holyoke. Homesickness settled heavily upon her again for a few days, but soon she was able to lose herself in her studies and friendships with fellow students and teachers. That winter she studied chemistry and physiology (the study of how human and animal organisms function), and wrote two compositions every month. Miss Lyon continued to encourage her toward professing her faith, and Emily continued to resist.

At the end of January came a break between terms. Emily again joyfully returned home. Coming back to Mount Holyoke afterward was harder than ever; she couldn't stop thinking about home and her family. She wrote to Austin, "Home was always dear to me & dearer still the friends around it, but never did it seem so dear as now. . . . when tempted to feel sad, I think of the blazing fire, & the cheerful meal & the chair empty now I am gone. I can hear the cheerful voices & the merry laugh & a desolate feeling comes home to my heart, to think I am alone."

In spite of its intensity, this bout of homesickness was a little easier to bear: her father had decided that Emily would not return to Mount Holyoke in the autumn. We don't know why he made this decision. Was it because of her homesickness? Did he fear for her health? Or, proud though he was of Emily's intellect, did he deem further studies less necessary for his daughter than for his son? Maybe he just wanted his family under one roof again. Whatever the reason, Emily was happy, counting down the weeks until she could return home for good. She would be especially glad to leave behind the pressure from Miss Lyon—and many of her fellow students—to declare herself for Christ.

Emily didn't feel well much of the winter, but she didn't let her parents know. She wanted to get through to the end of the term. Her cough grew so bad by March, though, that a visiting Amherst friend reported it to her parents. Edward immediately sent Austin to bring her home. She spent six weeks recovering in Amherst. Luckily spring vacation took up some of those six weeks, so she missed only four weeks of her studies. She did her best to keep up with them at home and was also delighted to greet the spring wildflowers in Amherst. By then she was well enough to enjoy pleasant rambles with friends to gather trailing arbutus, yellow violets, and bloodroot.

Back in May for her final term, Emily studied astronomy and rhetoric (using language to persuade an audience) and cut her piano practice down to one hour a day. Soon she could count the weeks left at Mount Holyoke on one hand.

Emily's last day at Mount Holyoke finally arrived. Commencement was held on August 3, 1848. In the crowded hall, she was amazed to glimpse the face of her old friend Abiah. Overjoyed, she waited for the ceremony to be over so she could go to her. To her great surprise and dismay, she could find no trace of her friend after the ceremony. How could Abiah have left Mount Holyoke without talking with her? Had Emily just imagined seeing her? Or did Abiah no longer consider Emily, who had last written to her in May, her friend? Emily was so upset by this thought that she couldn't bring herself to write to Abiah again for several months.

A MERRY LIFE
IN AMHERST

While Emily was feeling doubts about Abiah when she returned home to Amherst, she was very pleased that her friendship with Jane Humphrey could flourish again. Jane had been at Mount Holyoke the same year as Emily. She had been in the Senior Class, though, so the two girls' paths didn't often cross. But now Jane had graduated and had come to teach at Amherst Academy. The two spent much time in each other's company. They sat together in the front doorway of the Dickinson home after school, just as they had when they were young schoolgirls together.

Jane's presence was a special joy to Emily, but her old friend was just one part of Emily's busy social life. Austin was in his third year at Amherst College, and his friends often filled the Dickinson household. Emily's days were crowded with teas, evening calls, promenades, parties, lectures, concerts, and carriage rides. The young men from the college were a literary bunch, so there were many book discussions and much music. Often it was Emily who played the piano. There was even a Shakespeare Club.

In February 1849, Emily and her friends celebrated Valentine's Day. In the mid-1800s the holiday stretched over the entire week leading to February 14. It was not focused as much on romance as it is now; instead it was an occasion for young people to send cards, clever letters, and gifts to each other. This February, one of Austin's Amherst friends, William Cowper Dickinson (no relation), sent Emily a bestselling novel of the times, about an Italian prisoner, desperately lonely until he notices a plant growing in the prison courtyard. He tends to the plant, even naming it, and it becomes his only companion.

Emily thanked William in a letter, noting that she had felt a kinship with the solitary prisoner. This might have seemed strange, surrounded as she was by friends and family. Somewhere in her inner spirit, she was beginning to feel separated from those she loved.

Soon after Emily returned from Mount Holyoke, she made an important new friend. Benjamin Franklin Newton was a law student working in her father's office. His and Emily's friendship blossomed as she settled back into Amherst life. Emily thought of Benjamin, who was nine years older, as both a teacher and an older brother.

He was a frequent visitor to the Dickinson household. On those visits, he and Emily often talked about religious and spiritual matters and about nature. She came to deeply admire his thinking and intelligence. He recommended authors for her to read and lent her books.

When Benjamin left Amherst to continue his studies in Worcester, a city more than 50 miles away, Emily was greatly saddened. Soon after he left he sent her a copy of the first volume of poems written by the philosopher and essayist Ralph Waldo Emerson. Emerson's ideas and writings were becoming popular at the time and were the focus of much discussion in intellectual circles. Emily had read Emerson's essays, which stressed that a person should rely on his or her own direct experience above anything else. He believed that one should disregard external authority and trust one's own judgment. Emily's struggles about accepting Christ fit very well into this way of thinking.

Emerson's essays were the foundation of a philosophy that became known as transcendentalism. Transcendentalists believed that all beings were part of a larger soul, a Supreme Mind, and related to every tiny piece of the universe. Their motto was "Trust Thyself." Emerson's writings played an important role in shaping Emily's ideas. She was very pleased to receive the poetry book from Benjamin and declared it "beautiful." She and Benjamin continued to write to each other. He was the first of several older men Emily would look to for spiritual and intellectual guidance throughout her life.

Books also came to Emily from her father's law partner, Elbridge Bowdoin. He liked to lend both Emily and Vinnie novels—which their father, like many people at that time, did not approve of. (When Austin got hold of a popular novel, *Kavanagh* by Henry Wadsworth Longfellow, he had to sneak it into the house. He and Emily kept it hidden under the piano cover.) It was thanks to Bowdoin that Emily read one of the most popular novels of the day, *Jane Eyre.* When it was published in England in 1847, under the byline Currer Bell (later revealed to be the female Charlotte Brontë), one critic wrote that it made "the pulses gallop and heart beat."

Emily enjoyed *Jane Eyre* tremendously. When she returned the book to Bowdoin, she included a note expressing her wish that C.B. would write many more books.

Emily liked *Jane Eyre* so much that when Edward gave her a dog, a big brown Newfoundland, in the fall of 1849, she named him Carlo after a dog in that novel. Carlo was a friendly, curious, and intelligent dog. He quickly became Emily's companion on her frequent walks in the woods.

Another young man who came often to the Dickinsons' home was Joseph Lyman, Austin's friend from his days at Williston. When Austin had returned to Amherst in 1846, Joseph came with him. The Dickinsons all enjoyed his company, and Edward invited him to stay with the family until he went to Yale University later that year. Now attending the college in New Haven,

Connecticut, Joseph often returned to what he thought of as his second home.

A year older than Emily, Joseph found her to be a good conversationalist who shared his interest in literature. They read plays together and pored over the *American Dictionary of the English Language* by one-time Amherst resident Noah Webster. (Webster, like Emily's grandfather, had helped found Amherst College.) Joseph admitted that he found the conversation of most young women dull, but Emily was an exception. In a letter to his brother he wrote that Emily "is a year younger it is true but older than all in mind and heart."

His relationship with Vinnie, on the other hand, was decidedly romantic. When he first stayed with the Dickinsons, he would walk 13-year-old Vinnie to Amherst Academy, carrying her books and later helping her with her Latin. As she grew older, Vinnie was always at his side. She liked to sit in his lap, loosen her

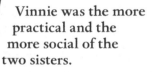

Vinnie was the more practical and the more social of the two sisters.

long brown hair, and playfully tie it around his neck. Joseph admired her soft skin and proclaimed himself "very very happy" with Vinnie.

In the autumn of 1849, though, now that she was 16, it was Vinnie's turn to leave home. She was sent more than 100 miles east to Ipswich Female Seminary, on the coastline north of Boston. In spite of all the good times with Amherst friends, Emily missed her sister terribly. Jane Humphrey was gone again, too, to teach in the town of Warren, about 25 miles south of Amherst, and in one of Emily's many letters to Jane, she complained of being left all alone. "The grave opened—and swallowed you both," she wrote.

So Emily especially enjoyed the Christmas vacation that year, with the whole family together again. Austin was not entirely free from studying; he had to finish reading a long history book. When he finally did, it was cause for celebration, which started with many friends taking part in a sleigh ride.

On New Year's Eve, Emily, Austin, and Vinnie gathered with about 20 friends to welcome 1850. They played music and charades, shared supper, then talked and walked together until two in the morning. To their surprise, they all felt fine the next day! The parties continued until the vacation came to an end with Vinnie's departure for Ipswich.

Soon after that, Emily wrote her uncle Joel Norcross a long letter about the fun she was having that season: "Amherst is alive with fun this winter . . . sleigh rides

are as plenty as people . . . beaus can be had for the taking . . . maids smile like the mornings in June." Early
in the new year, Abiah finally made a weeklong visit to
Amherst, and she and Emily revived their friendship.
Soon they were exchanging letters again, as in earlier
years.

As another Valentine's Day approached, Emily joined
in her crowd's spirit of competition as to who could com-
pose the cleverest Valentine verses. She sent a silly little
verse to William Cowper Dickinson, illustrated with
small pictures cut out from old books and papers. It was
hardly valentine-like in tone: "Life is but a strife - /️ T'is
a bubble - / T'is a dream - / And man is but a little *boat*
/ Which paddles down the stream."

She also composed a much longer valentine, even
more nonsensical, that was published in the Amherst
College literary magazine, the *Indicator*. The first of her
writing to be published, it appeared anonymously, as did
all of Emily's work published during her lifetime, with
the title "Valentine Eve." Beginning "Magnum bonum,
'harum scarum', zounds et zounds, et war alarum,
man reformam, life perfectum, mundum changum, all
things flarum?" it went on to say "Sir, I desire an inter-
view; meet me at sunrise, or sunset, or the new moon
- the place is immaterial." It ran in the Editor's Corner,
with a note from the issue's editor, Henry Shipley, reading: "I wish I knew who the author is. I think she must
have some spell, by which she quickens the imagination
and causes the high blood 'run frolic through the veins.'"

The valentine was not unlike a lot of the writing that filled Emily's letters to family and friends. She wrote extended metaphors—some that went on for pages—about things as ordinary as catching a cold. Sometimes she related strange dreams; often she reflected on the passage of time. While Emily was not writing poetry yet, her letters show an imagination in full literary bloom. Many notes to close friends like Abiah and Jane read like love letters, filled with longing for their presence.

Looking at the number and length of the letters Emily wrote, it may seem that she was obsessed with her correspondence. But letter writing in the mid-1800s was not only a way of communicating with friends and relatives; it was also considered an important part of a person's education.

In the first half of 1850, Emily's letters were again filled with religious and spiritual contemplations. She was responding to the great religious fervor that began sweeping through Amherst and other New England towns that February. When Emily had left Mount Holyoke at the end of 1848, she had left behind the relentless pressure from Mary Lyon, as well as other teachers and most fellow students, to profess her faith. But now religious zeal surrounded her again, even more strongly. Mary Lyon's persuasions had been always gentle, if firm. The residents of Amherst were ardent. They filled churches and turned their souls over to God.

"Christ is calling everyone here," Emily wrote to Jane in the first days of April, "all my companions have answered." Abby Wood, who had long resisted the call together with Emily, now answered it. Even Vinnie, at Ipswich, had turned to Christ. Of all the Dickinsons, only Austin remained "without hope" with Emily; in May their father professed his faith. (Their mother had done so long ago, when the children were all still young.)

Emily felt the familiar conflict. She tried to explain it to Jane: "I can't tell you *what* they have found, but *they* think it is something precious. . . . It *certainly* comes from God—and I think to receive it is blessed—not that I know it from *me*, but from those on whom *change* has passed. They seem so very tranquil, and their voices are kind, and gentle, and the tears fill their eyes so often, I really think I envy them." She asked Jane to pray for her that she too might be led to God. But she struggled to understand just how she would hear and understand this call from Christ. She asked Abiah to please try to explain it to her. We don't know how Abiah responded, but Emily—in spite of eventually writing many poems about God—was never able to bring herself to answer the call.

Vinnie's absence meant more than loneliness for Emily. It also meant that she had to spend much more time on household chores. Other than baking, Emily did not enjoy household work. The situation grew especially bad in May, when her mother was taken ill with acute neuralgia (a damaged nerve in the face and neck). Emily was forced to take up cooking and cleaning. She tried to do it all with good humor. Late one morning, though, while she was washing dishes and a friend stopped by to invite her to ride in the woods, it felt like the last straw. She had dishes to wash. She had to turn him down.

Once her mother was improving, Emily looked forward to less housework. She shocked herself by referring to "my kitchen" in a letter to Abiah, writing, "God forbid that it was, or shall be my own—God keep me from what they call households!"

When the school term ended that summer, Vinnie came home for good. But Austin graduated from Amherst on August 30, and in September he left for a teaching job in Sunderland, a few miles north of Amherst. It seemed to Emily that as soon as one sibling returned, the other left. Would she ever live with both her brother and sister again?

There was a silver lining in Emily's life, though: she had a new friend, Susan Gilbert. Susan had briefly attended Amherst Academy in 1847. The Gilbert girls (there were four in all, plus two brothers) had lost their parents when they were children. Susan and Martha, being the two youngest, had lived briefly with their married sister, Harriet Cutler, in Amherst and then with an aunt in Geneva, New York. Now they had returned to settle in with Harriet. Susan was just nine days younger than Emily, and a friendship quickly blossomed. Of all the friends dear to Emily's heart, Susan was the one whose life would become most deeply intertwined with hers.

But it was to her friend Jane that Emily confided something new and very important in her life. Even as she wrote of her conflicting religious feelings, she turned to another subject. She wrote with great excitement, but vaguely, as though she were afraid to express exactly what was happening. "I have dared to do strange things," she began, "bold things, and have asked no advice from any—I have heeded beautiful tempters, yet do not think I am wrong."

She longs to sit down with Jane and confess to "an experience bitter, and sweet, but the sweet did so beguile me—and life has had an aim, and the world has been too precious for your poor—and striving sister!" She wrote that things were "budding, and springing, and singing." Jane could probably make no sense of what Emily was trying to tell her. But most scholars agree that Emily, at the age of 19, was trying to describe her first attempts at writing poetry.

EMILY AT TWENTY

Emily may have been experimenting with writing poetry in the first years of the new decade, but other than the veiled hints to Jane, she kept her efforts to herself. She and Vinnie continued to lead a busy social life, usually together. Tuesday and Friday evenings the young people gathered for a reading circle, which sometimes ended with dancing.

The sisters' many outings often put their anxious father in an even more anxious state. One evening when Emily returned at 9:00 PM from visiting friends, she found Edward terribly upset at her long absence. Vinnie and their mother were in tears, worried at what he might do to Emily when she did finally get home. Emily herself was somewhat amused by his agitation. She had learned to take her father's nervous nature in stride.

Emily was now a young woman of 20. She had auburn hair, with eyes of similar hue, soft and warm. She was always neatly and carefully dressed. Among strangers she was usually a little shy and quiet, but with friends she was direct and kind and exuded a spirit of fun. She didn't lack for attention from the young men who attended Amherst College. Her frequent companions included George Gould, one of the editors of the college's *Indicator* magazine; Henry Vaughan Emmons, with whom she loved to go riding and talk about books; and a distant cousin, John Graves, who often visited with Henry.

But Emily was closest to her female friends, like Sue Gilbert and her sister Martha, her former Amherst Academy schoolmate Emily Fowler, faraway Abiah, and Jane Humphrey. She and her dear girlhood friend Abby Wood had lost some of their closeness after Abby had turned to Christ. They now looked at life differently, Emily felt. Most important of all for Emily was her bond with Vinnie and Austin—especially Austin. Emily and her brother shared the same sense of humor and witty tongue, as well as a passion for nature and reading.

When Austin was home, part of Emily's morning routine was to pop into his bedroom to wake him up. When he was away, the very sight of his empty room in the mornings made her lonely. The teaching job in Sunderland hadn't gone well, and he was home by

Thanksgiving. But in June 1851 he left again in hopes of a better experience at a school in Boston.

The entire family mourned his absence. Edward, Emily wrote Austin in a letter soon after his departure, "is as uneasy when you are gone away as if you catch a trout, and put him in Sahara" (her clever version of "a fish out of water"). He included Austin in their daily morning prayers while their mother wiped her eyes with a corner of her apron. Their mother, Emily also noted, worried about how he was getting his washing done. A little boy named Austin Grout came by daily to pick a basket of the Dickinsons' ripe cherries, and their mother enjoyed addressing him by name, to remind herself of her absent son. And Vinnie liked to occasionally comment, "Did'nt we have a *brother* - it seems to me we *did* - his name was Austin - we call, but

Austin Dickinson in 1850, when he was 21 years old.

he answers not again." Sometimes, setting the table for dinner, Emily mistakenly laid five places. Removing one brought a tear to her eye.

Austin's letters from Boston were eagerly awaited. When Edward picked one up at the post office, he read it immediately, no matter who it was addressed to. Then he had Emily read it aloud at the dinner table. In the evening, he would sit down, crack a few walnuts, put on his glasses, and read it to himself again. The letters were full of humor and often left all four of the Dickinsons reeling with laughter.

One of Austin's very first letters from Boston urged his sisters to come visit that summer. The country was buzzing about the visit of a celebrated Swedish singer, soprano Jenny Lind. Known as the "Swedish Nightingale," she had captured the hearts of Europeans with her pure and natural voice. Now she was touring the United States and would soon be in Boston. Emily and Vinnie were eager to come—as much to see their brother as to hear the singer—and began planning their trip. Later in June they had to write with the bad news that they couldn't come, after all. The dressmaker was scheduled to arrive, as was their grandmother. If they traveled to Boston, they would have to return home immediately after the concert, instead of staying for a longer visit. They promised they would come soon.

As luck would have it, the sisters were not deprived of the chance to hear Jenny Lind sing. After Boston, her tour brought her to Northampton, less than eight miles from

Amherst. It was a long trip for a concert, but it was rare for an international artist to visit western Massachusetts. At 6:00 PM on the evening of July 4, the Dickinson sisters and their parents set out by carriage for Northampton.

The concert wasn't scheduled to begin until 8:00 PM, but the family wisely left extra time for the trip. Halfway to Northampton, they began to hear thunder. Soon a suspicious-looking cloud appeared in the sky. And then the skies opened and sheets of rain fell on the carriage. The Dickinsons arrived, drenched, at a Northampton hotel, hoping to wait out the rain. But it continued to fall, and so they walked in the downpour to Edwards Church, where Lind's performance was to take place.

But it was all worth it. The singing was like nothing the audience had ever heard before. Emily wrote Austin that it wasn't the singing they loved but Jenny Lind herself, with her foreign accent, her blue eyes, and her sweet and touching nature, like a child's, Emily thought. The "boquets fell in showers," Emily wrote, "and the roof was rent with applause—how it thundered outside, and inside with the thunder of God and of men."

Edward, however, didn't seem to know how to respond to such a performance. He sat throughout it with a silly, angry expression on his face that made Emily laugh. She realized that for her Puritanical father, the experience was too extreme. Emily wanted to write Austin all about the concert that very night, but they returned home after midnight. She had to wait until Sunday to pen her detailed description of the evening.

Emily's love of music had first been noted by Aunt Lavinia when Emily, just two years old, learned to play the piano; her passion continued into her early adulthood. While both she and Vinnie often entertained their parents or their friends by playing the piano, Emily's favorite time at the instrument was late at night. After everybody had gone to bed, she would slip downstairs. As the household slept, she would improvise her own melodies. Overnight visitors were sometimes awakened by the sounds of her musical inventions. Emily happily took whatever opportunities came her way to hear other musicians perform, so hearing Jenny Lind was a special treat.

Jenny Lind's concert was not the only excitement that summer. Later that month, in the middle of one afternoon, a fire broke out in a neighbor's barn. Amherst was in the midst of a dry spell, and a westerly wind was blowing, so the blaze quickly spread to several nearby homes, including a small house that Edward owned. Edward immediately took charge, marshaling a group of men who were able to get the fire under control and put it out. The barn where the fire had started was burned to the ground, but the other buildings suffered only some damage to their roofs. Edward was cheered as the hero and even more so when he arranged for the local inn's restaurant to host all the firefighters.

Otherwise, the summer was a generally pleasant one, even though both Emily and Vinnie did not feel completely well. Both sisters had a cough, and Emily had lost weight. Their plans to visit Austin had to be put off again because Edward didn't think they were strong enough to travel. They had hoped to consult a Boston doctor whom their aunt Lavinia relied on. But Edward insisted they stay in Amherst under the care of Dr. Brewster, a local doctor he had great faith in. When Brewster failed to cure them, Edward decided to take them to the nearby town of Greenfield, where there was another doctor he trusted deeply.

The situation was frustrating for Emily and Vinnie. They were well enough to do their chores, have company, and go out with their friends, but not well enough for their father to let them travel. Emily thought that if she could just see Austin, that would cure her. After a few weeks, they finally began to feel much better. Learning that Austin was coming home for a short visit cheered everybody. Emily and Vinnie made currant wine; their mother baked more pies than usual. The garden was overflowing with beets, beans, and potatoes, and the apples were starting to ripen. Emily was eager for conversation with her brother and wrote him, "I arrange my tho'ts in a convenient shape." Describing her sister's state of mind, Emily wrote, "Vinnie grows only *perter* and *more* pert day by day."

August also brought Abiah Root to town. Emily spotted her at the Amherst College Commencement, an important annual event that drew many visitors. Especially significant for the Dickinsons, who had been so instrumental in the founding of the college,

Commencement included a variety of activities and important speakers. The Dickinsons hosted an afternoon reception at their home every year in honor of the celebration. When she grew older, Emily often served the guests sherry from the family's large glass decanter at these gatherings.

Emily hadn't known Abiah was coming, so she was delightfully surprised to see her. It had been a long time since the two had been together. The girls spoke briefly, and Emily looked forward to spending time with her the next day. She couldn't wait to sit and talk with Abiah about important things—she wanted to get Abiah's thoughts about "eternal feelings—how things *beyond* are to you," she wrote her later. She hoped to explore with her friend "what we were, and what we *are* and may be."

But evidently Abiah was not as eager to talk with Emily. The next morning, Emily was disappointed to find that Abiah had already left town. Emily wrote her a long emotional letter, expressing her frustration at the state of their friendship. It's not clear why Abiah was avoiding Emily, but that seemed to be her intent. It's possible that Emily's long, impassioned letters felt overwhelming to Abiah, or Abiah may have felt distant from her old friend because of their differing views on religion.

It was hard for Emily to believe that the long friendship with Abiah might be over. But she was warmed by the deepening bond between herself and Sue Gilbert. Over the summer she had come to spend more time with Sue than with any other girl in town. Sue's sister Martha had also become close to both Emily and Vinnie.

Sue, however, was growing increasingly uncomfortable being supported by her older sister Harriet Cutler and Harriet's husband. She decided, against the wishes of her family and friends (especially Emily), to take a teaching job in Baltimore, Maryland. In September, she left Amherst. With both Austin and Sue far away, Emily devoted even more time to her correspondence. She wrote more letters in 1851 and 1852 than she had in the nine previous years.

Soon after Sue left, Emily and Vinnie finally made their trip to Boston. It was a hot September in the city, and they were unaccustomed to the smoke and dust, but being with Austin made up for any discomfort. The sisters stayed with Aunt Lavinia, who by now had two daughters—Loo was nine years old, and Frances, called Fanny, had just turned four.

After two busy weeks enjoying the company of their brother, aunt, and little cousins, they set out for home. While their time in Boston had been pleasant, they—especially Emily—felt Amherst and their circle of friends was far superior to the city and its inhabitants.

Emily and Vinnie felt sorry to leave Austin behind there, alone. They could console each other in his absence, but Austin had nobody to comfort him for being away from his family. "Home is a holy thing . . ." Emily wrote him, "I feel it more and more as the great world goes on."

Although Sue was not in Amherst to greet Emily and Vinnie, Martha Gilbert was. They were very happy to see her. Austin had sent Martha a gift of a bracelet, and Emily had some fun pretending it was her own. She opened up the little box and showed Martha the pretty beads. Then Emily put the bracelet on her wrist, and Martha further admired it. Taking the bracelet off, Emily clasped it on Martha's wrist and, as Martha oohed and aahed at its beauty, Emily confessed that it was actually a gift from Austin for Martha. Martha was overcome with joy.

Meanwhile Austin was also keeping up a warm correspondence with Sue. He seemed to be publicly enjoying the long-distance company of both Gilbert sisters, just as he had enjoyed it in Amherst. This did not seem out of the ordinary to anybody. Martha would bring Sue's letters asking about Austin to read to Emily and Vinnie; Emily would write to Austin about Sue's letters and send Martha's love to him. With Sue away, Emily and Vinnie spent more and more time with Martha and were coming to love her as much as they loved Sue. The sisters encouraged Austin in both friendships.

Emily's letters to her friends often overflowed with passion, but her letters to Sue in Baltimore that year are particularly passionate. It's tempting to consider them love letters when reading phrases such as: "Susie, forgive me darling . . . my heart is full of you, none other than you in my thoughts." Emily was expressing the intense feelings that overwhelmed her when the people she cared for were absent.

Emily's letters were an important part of her development as a writer. As she took her first steps into writing poetry, she was also trying out different styles of writing in her correspondence. (For many years she also liked to vary her signature from *Emily* to *Emilie* to *Emily E.D.*) To Austin she might describe the domestic details of a Sunday evening at home or lyrically render the beauty of an October afternoon: "you will find the blue hills, Austin, with the autumnal shadows silently sleeping on them, and there will be a glory lingering around the day." Evocative descriptions such as these trace Emily's growing love of nature imagery. But she also related incidents with great humor and continued to create elaborate extended metaphors that turned otherwise mundane subjects into fanciful tales.

On December 10, 1851, Emily celebrated her 21st birthday with Martha, Abby Wood, and Abiah, who was visiting Amherst again. The girls, along with Vinnie, had a pleasant tea together. Austin was much missed, but the gifts he sent—books and piano music—were admired and appreciated.

Christmas and then the new year arrived quietly, with Emily looking forward to the time when both Austin and Sue would be back in Amherst. Busy as her life was with friends, music, gardening, and household work—and of course, her correspondence—her world never felt complete when the people she loved were far from her.

7

A BUDDING POET

I n February 1852 Emily had big news to send Austin:
the long-hoped-for building of a railroad was finally
going to occur! There was no railroad line through
Amherst, and Edward had been leading the effort to
bring train service to the town for what seemed like
forever. That month, the decision was finalized to build
the Amherst and Belchertown railroad, and Edward was
to be one of the directors of the company. There was
great rejoicing throughout the neighboring towns, and
their father, Emily wrote Austin, was full of "excessive
satisfaction." She wished that Austin was there with his
"big Hurrahs." Celebrations were so much more exciting when Austin, tall with his unruly reddish hair, was
part of them.

February also saw the usual flurry of Valentine's Day notes and poems. To Emily's surprise, her valentine to young William Howland, who had worked in her father's law firm, was published, anonymously, in the February 20, 1852, issue of the *Springfield Daily Republican* newspaper. The valentine, a poem of 17 quatrains (verses with four lines) with the second and fourth lines of each verse rhyming, holds two mysteries. First, to this day nobody knows who sent it to the newspaper. (Although it's interesting to note that Howland had recently started his own law practice in Springfield.)

Second, Emily never showed any special interest in Howland. Why she chose him as the recipient of this long poem is mystifying. While Edward enjoyed Howland's company and invited him home often, neither Emily nor Vinnie were particularly taken with him. A few months earlier, in fact, Howland had made a marriage proposal to Vinnie, who, finding his company boring, turned him down.

The ambitious poem is noteworthy for being so cleverly written and technically well done. "Sic transit gloria mundi" it began in Latin, continuing "'How doth the busy bee' / Dum vivamus vivamus / I stay mine enemy! —" That 21-year-old Emily would take the time and effort to execute this long work shows that poetry writing was beginning to occupy an important place in her life.

That winter Amherst residents experienced more bad health than usual. Luckily neither Emily nor Vinnie fell ill, but Martha was hit so hard by the flu that she couldn't write to Austin for weeks. Emily sent him warm messages from Martha in her own letters. Abby Wood, with whom Emily was starting to feel closer again, was also sick. Emily couldn't help thinking about her childhood friend Abby Haskell, who had died just last spring. She also remembered two other girls, both about her age, who had died just a few months earlier, in October. Consumption continued to be a frequent cause of death, especially among young people. Medicine in the mid-1800s was not sophisticated enough to help those who were weak and frail.

The weather didn't help. A heavy snowstorm in January halted mail delivery. February was marked by more snow, then rain and wind. Vinnie and Emily mostly stayed in and chatted while Vinnie sewed and Emily wrote letters to Sue and Austin. One day in February they talked about growing old. Emily found it humorous that Vinnie, not yet 19, feared the thought of turning 20. The sisters tried to master a piano composition for four hands that Austin had sent from Boston entitled "Duett," but Vinnie couldn't learn it. Emily asked Austin to exchange it for something simpler.

Emily didn't mind the bad weather when it fell on a Sunday. Her father still worried about her health more than about the others'. She was prone to lingering coughs and lost weight easily. Edward didn't like her to attend church if it was rainy or windy or cold. Emily was happy to stay home and pour out her heart on paper to Sue.

She missed Sue so much that sometimes she would read Sue's letters to visiting friends and even talked about her to ones who didn't know her. For Emily and Martha, Sue was a constant topic of conversation.

As spring approached, it began to feel like illness wouldn't leave them. In March Edward came down with rheumatism (which causes stiffness, pain, and swelling in a person's joints and muscles), and in May Emily's mother had another attack of neuralgia. Emily impatiently counted down the months, then weeks, and finally days until Sue would return to Amherst in early July, followed by Austin later that month.

In June Edward was elected as a delegate to the Whig convention in Baltimore. He had been a strong member of this new political party since it had been formed in 1834. The Whig Party was founded in response to the election of Andrew Jackson as president. The Whigs believed that Jackson took on too much power, acting more like a king than a president. Since 1834 the party had had several successes in electing Whig candidates to the White House, and some failures, too.

The convention this year—1852—was especially important. The party was already divided by opposing views on slavery held by members from the North and South. It was beginning to lose Southerners to the Democratic Party, which supported individual states being able to make their own laws about slavery. For Edward, a staunch Whig, being part of this momentous convention was a mark of great distinction.

For Emily, Edward's trip to Baltimore served as an opportunity for her father to personally deliver a letter to Sue. Even though Sue would be back in Amherst in less than one month, in that letter Emily lamented that she, too, wanted to attend the convention. "Why can't I be a Delegate to the great Whig Convention?" she wrote. "Then, Susie I could see you, during a pause in the session." She enclosed violets, one of her favorite flowers, in the letter. Edward, who was fond of Sue, was glad to have the opportunity to pay her a visit and deliver Emily's letter.

By June good health had returned to all. Parties were being thrown on a regular basis. Emily, boasting a new haircut (Vinnie thought Emily looked very pretty with the short hair), attended one given by Abby Wood and looked forward to a few others. Vinnie was even more social, going to nearly all of them. "Amherst is growing lively," Emily informed Austin, "and by the time you come, everything will be in

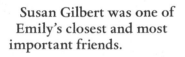

Susan Gilbert was one of Emily's closest and most important friends.

a buzz." Martha sent her love to Austin as always, but Emily reported to him that Mr. Bowdoin (their father's law clerk), had developed a fancy for Martha. He called on her several times a day. Martha, noted Emily, had taken to smiling and looking a little peculiar whenever Bowdoin's name was mentioned.

With Sue's arrival imminent, Emily could think of nothing else. Even in church her mind was preoccupied. What should she wear to welcome Sue home? She was torn between her fawn-colored dress and a blue one. She decided finally on the blue. Emily and Martha had recently had several deep heart-to-heart talks about love, marriage, children, and death. Emily longed to have those talks with Sue. She felt that in spite of their close friendship, they hadn't delved into those really important things.

Vinnie also felt very close to the Gilbert sisters, though her practical nature kept her from expressing herself in the more ardent words Emily liked to use. She told Emily (and Emily wrote Sue), "I dont know but it's wrong, but I love Sue . . . and Mattie better than all the friends I ever had in my life." In her letter, Emily added, "Vinnie hopes to be like you, and to do as you do."

By August, Emily's heart was full. Sue and Austin were both settled at home again; her garden was still in bloom. The late-summer gentian and crimson-red lobelia, which drew hummingbirds, had arrived. The orchard was heavy with peaches, pears, plums, and the promise of autumn apples and grapes.

It warmed Emily's heart, too, that Sue and Austin were growing closer. She loved both Martha and Sue and had supported Austin's attention toward the sisters. In his letters from Boston, Austin had first written affectionately and warmly to Martha, regarded by all as the gentler, sweeter sister. His letters to Sue, who was considered smarter, sharper, and livelier, were more flirtatious and, eventually, more emotional. When he began confiding his deeper thoughts and religious doubts to Martha, she stopped responding to his letters. His outpourings may have been overwhelming to her.

In Amherst both Martha and Sue were dependent on their sister Harriet Cutler and her husband. While they were grateful for the support, they found the stiff and overly heated Cutler home difficult to bear. Sue had had a year on her own in Baltimore, and by early 1853 Martha made her own escape from the Cutler household. She moved to Grand Haven, Michigan, where the Gilberts' two wealthy older brothers lived.

Sue may have found the Cutler home easier to bear now that she was becoming so much a part of the Dickinson household. Her relationship with Austin was secretly becoming romantic (although townspeople did note how often the two were together at public events). Sue lent him her copy of a book of love sonnets by the English poet Elizabeth Barrett Browning. She marked the passages she especially wanted him to read, the ones that expressed her own feelings.

It wasn't long before Emily, and then Vinnie, too, were let in on their secret. The Dickinson parents, though unaware of the change in Austin and Sue's relationship, took Sue in wholeheartedly. Emily believed that they were coming to feel that "she is their's just as much" as Vinnie, Austin, and herself. Often Edward would walk Sue home in the evening. Emily noted to Austin, "I think Father feels that she appreciates him, better than most anybody else."

By the time Sue went to visit friends in New Hampshire in February 1853, she and Austin were secretly engaged—though Emily knew everything. Signing off one of her letters to Sue in New Hampshire, she corrected herself from sending "my" mother's and sister's love, to "*thy* mother and thy sister . . . Susie . . . !"

Before Sue had returned from her visit, Austin, done with his teaching experiments, left for Cambridge in March to begin studying at Harvard Law School. Emily gave him several envelopes addressed to Sue in her own handwriting, so that he could write to his beloved without anybody suspecting the letters came from him. Emily enjoyed being part of the couple's intrigue. She even helped them set up a secret meeting at a hotel in Boston, and when gossip about the meeting got out, she helped quiet it down.

After the sweet months of having Austin and Sue in Amherst, and witnessing their love bloom, Emily—even with Vinnie's company—felt alone again. Their absences

felt harder to bear now than when Sue had been in Baltimore and Austin in Boston. "This is a lonely house,
when we are not all here," she wrote Austin.

Still, the Dickinson household was never without guests. Emily and Vinnie continued to entertain
friends like Henry Vaughan Emmons and John Graves.
Emily was sometimes reluctant to entertain on her
own, though. Vinnie liked to go out more than Emily
did, and on occasions when Vinnie planned to be else-
where, Emily didn't hesitate to cancel guests. One February evening she let John and Henry know that since
Vinnie wouldn't be home, "it will not be as pleasant."
She invited them to come and taste their currant wine
the following week, when both sisters could entertain
them.

Emily was coming to rely on Vinnie more and more,
in both social and practical matters. When Vinnie's right
hand was bitten by a neighbor's dog she tried to pet—
and the injury was so bad that Vinnie fainted from the
pain—all the housework fell to Emily. What's more, she
had to comb Vinnie's hair and help her to dress each day.
She couldn't help feeling a little overwhelmed by all the
responsibilities.

Though few were aware of it, Emily was devoting
herself more and more to her poetry. There are very
few examples of her poems from the early 1850s, but she
included one in a letter to Sue in New Hampshire that
winter:

Write! Comrade, write!

On this wondrous sea
Sailing, silently,
Ho! Pilot! ho!
Knowest thou the shore
Where no breakers roar -
Where the storm is oer?

In the peaceful west
Many the sails at rest -
The anchors fast -
Thither I pilot *thee* -
Land Ho! Eternity!
Ashore at last!
    Emilie–

A letter to Austin written soon after the one to Sue reveals clearer evidence that writing poetry was becoming important to her. Emily responded to Austin's declaration that he had been writing some poetry. First she made fun of him for his endeavors. But then she made her own admission: "Now, Brother Pegasus, I'll tell you what it is—I've been in the habit *myself* of writing some few things, and it rather appears to me that you're getting away my patent, so you'd better be somewhat careful, or I'll call the police!"

She wrote in a joking tone, but beneath the humor was a strong feeling of ownership. Emily was already seeing herself as a poet, as *the* poet of the Dickinson family. She didn't want to share that role with her brother, who in so many ways was the celebrity of the family. She was clearly telling Austin that poetry was her territory and he should stay out of it.

Warning Austin away from poetry did not mean that she missed him any less. She was also deeply affected by the news that Benjamin Franklin Newton had died in Worcester. Benjamin had been a warm friend and teacher. He had introduced her to many important writers and thinkers just a few years earlier, and she had learned a great deal from him. "Oh Austin," she wrote her brother, "Newton is dead. The first of my own friends. Pace [Peace]." While Emily had many friends, this phrase reveals that Benjamin's friendship was the first that engaged her intellect and deep reflection.

Emily was so shaken by Benjamin's death that she wrote to his minister in Worcester. She introduced herself and her relationship to the deceased, describing him as "a gentle, yet grave Preceptor . . . an elder brother, loved indeed." She wanted to know if he had died peacefully and was now "at Home . . . in Heaven." Far too many of Emily's girlhood friends had died, but Benjamin was the first close teacher she lost, and she mourned him very differently.

Also deeply important to her was that Benjamin had believed she could become a poet—the first person in her life to express that faith in her when her need to write was just budding. Now that she was seriously considering poetry as her calling in life, Benjamin's early belief in her talent was especially meaningful.

8

A SECOND SISTER

Amherst celebrated a milestone on June 9, 1853: the railroad was completed. On that day a passenger train made its first trip from New London, Connecticut, more than 100 miles away, to Amherst. Edward Dickinson was again the hero for bringing the railroad to town. He had not only led the effort but also invested a lot of money in it. As he marched through town "Like some old Roman General, upon a Triumph Day," wrote Emily, she herself stole off to the woods. Seeing the train roar into Amherst that day may have inspired one of her most famous later poems.

> I like to see it lap the Miles -
> And lick the Valleys up -

And stop to feed itself at Tanks -
And then - prodigious step

Around a Pile of Mountains -
And supercilious peer
In Shanties - by the sides of Roads -
And then a Quarry pare

To fit it's sides
And crawl between
Complaining all the while
In horrid - hooting stanza -
Then chase itself down Hill -

And neigh like Boanerges -
Then - prompter than a Star
Stop - docile and omnipotent
At it's own stable door -

The completion of the railroad was Edward's first triumph of 1853. The second came at the end of the year, in December, when he went off to Washington, DC, as the elected Whig representative for Massachusetts's 10th Congressional District. He was eager for his family to visit him in the spring. Vinnie and their mother were excited by the prospect, but Emily had no interest in leaving Amherst for a big noisy city—even for a short time—and Edward did not insist.

As the Dickinson household began to bustle with seamstresses and helpers of all kinds in preparation for the April trip, Emily was happy with her decision to stay home. She enjoyed her carriage rides with Henry Vaughan Emmons and their talks about books and poetry.

One of the poems that meant the most to Emily and Henry was Elizabeth Barrett Browning's "A Vision of Poets." More than 1,000 lines long, the poem explores how a poet is formed and the importance of not only love but also cruelty and suffering in creating a poet's vision. Browning invokes many renowned poets of the past. The result is a rich and inspiring celebration of the poet as visionary. This poem deeply influenced Emily, on the cusp of dedicating her life to this vocation. Browning remained one of Emily's favorite poets throughout her life; her portrait hung in Emily's bedroom until the day she died.

By spring, Austin and Sue's engagement was public news. Townspeople seemed to approve—one neighbor stopped by the Dickinsons' to comment how happy Emily and Vinnie must be to have such a beautiful sister. Edward responded with joy and pride that Sue would now be part of his family.

During Vinnie and their mother's trip to Washington, Sue stayed with Emily. Even though Emily was 23 years old, there was no question of her staying alone at home. Protective Edward was also worried about the young women being alone at night, so he asked John Graves to sleep in the house. Early during their stay, Sue and John were startled awake by Emily's nocturnal piano playing. Soon they got used to it, and John even came to enjoy it.

When summer came, Sue and Austin began planning
their marriage for the autumn of 1855. Austin graduated
from law school in July and returned to Amherst. It soon
became clear that the couple was thinking of leaving
Amherst for the Midwest, where Sue's two brothers had
been so successful. Emily was distraught at the prospect
of losing them.

Anxiety over her approaching marriage, a possible
major move, and growing tensions with Emily made Sue
ill. Everyone who tended to her, including a professional
nurse and other friends, worried over what seemed to
be a nervous breakdown. Eventually Sue's sister Harriet
decided Sue needed to leave Amherst to have any chance
of improving. She took Sue to their aunt's in Geneva,
New York.

After some time in Geneva, Sue traveled on to her
siblings in Michigan. Austin made an exploratory trip
to the Midwest to see what his professional prospects
might be there, eventually joining Sue in Michigan.
While he soon returned to Amherst, it was nearly six
months before Sue felt well enough to come back.

During these months of separation, Emily and Sue's
correspondence often took the form of an argument. Just
before Sue left in August, Emily wrote her about their
growing differences: "Sue, you can go or stay - There is
but one alternative - We differ often lately, and this must
be the last." While the letter talked about separation,
Emily enclosed a poem that showed an entirely different
side of her feelings:

I have a Bird in spring
Which for myself doth sing -
The spring decoys.
And as the summer nears -
And as the Rose appears,
Robin is gone.

Yet do I not repine
Knowing that Bird of mine
Though flown -
Learneth beyond the sea
Melody new for me
And will return.

Fast in a safer hand
Held in a truer Land
Are mine -
And though they now depart,
Tell I my doubting heart
They're thine.

In a serener Bright,
In a more golden light
I see
Each little doubt and fear,
Each little discord here
Removed.

Then will I not repine,
Knowing that Bird of mine

Though flown
Shall in a distant tree
Bright melody for me
Return.

In this poem, Emily expressed her faith that their separation would enrich Sue and that she (the "Bird" of the
poem) would return to Emily, their friendship revived.
The sharply worded letter taken together with the opti-
mistic poem reflects Emily's complex feelings toward
Sue. But mostly, it shows the depth of her need for Sue's
constant friendship.

The August 1854 Amherst Commencement held
some poignancy for Emily. She was losing another special friend. Henry, her literary and spiritual ally, was
graduating. Their many talks of books, poems, and
spiritual questions had inspired her as Benjamin had in
a similar fashion years earlier. The difference was that
Henry was not so much a teacher as an equal. Together
the two explored ideas about pain, solitude, the sacred-
ness of nature, and, of course, poetry. In addition to
books, they shared their writing with each other. Henry
was one of the first people with whom Emily shared her
own poems. (She referred to them as "flowers" in the
notes she wrote to him.)

Emily's friendship with Henry fed her growing devotion to poetry. She would miss him very much.

As her 24th birthday approached, changes were
afloat in Emily's world: Henry gone, Sue and Austin

to be married. But an even greater change was on the
horizon. In September 1854 David Mack, owner of the
Homestead, died. Emily's birthplace was now for sale.

9

BACK TO THE HOMESTEAD

E dward was eager to reclaim his family home. He made an offer of $6,000 for the house, the property surrounding it, and the 11-acre meadow across the street. By April 1855, the Homestead once again belonged to the Dickinsons. Edward was proud to be able to move his own family back to the house his father had built more than four decades earlier. He felt he was making up for the embarrassment of his father's failure to hold on to it. What's more, the Homestead was one of Amherst's most prominent properties. Edward believed his distinguished family belonged there.

Before the family could move in, much remodeling had to be done. A square cupola was added to the roof, and a large porch was put on the west side of the house.

8

A small extension was taken off the back of the house so that a much larger, two-story addition could be built, which included a new kitchen. For his wife and eldest daughter, Edward had a greenhouse built on the southeastern side of the house. Emily and her mother would now be able to tend to their plants even in the months of frost and snow.

Edward also had a proposal for Austin. He didn't want Austin and Sue—who had finally returned in February, healthy and accompanied by Martha—to move to the Midwest. The Dickinsons were an Amherst family. He invited Austin to join him as partner in his law practice. And he offered to build the couple a fine house, next

Edward extensively remodeled the Homestead before his family moved back in November 1855.

door to the Homestead. Austin initially hesitated, but Sue loved the idea of having her own home for the first time. Austin eventually warmed to the plan, especially since Edward allowed him to make all the decisions about the house's design. With a new house to build, Sue and Austin decided to postpone their wedding until the following spring.

During Sue's absence, Emily and Vinnie had been on a trip of their own. In February 1855 the sisters traveled to Washington, DC, to join their father while Congress was in session. Their three-week stay did not particularly impress Emily, although she marveled at the green grass and blooming maple trees of the city in late February. Occasionally she did not feel well enough to keep up with the busy city life, though she remarked that "I'm gayer than I was before." Vinnie, always the more social sister, enjoyed walking with female friends and befriending the other guests at the Willard Hotel. One springlike day, the sisters journeyed down the Potomac River by boat to visit Mount Vernon. Emily and Vinnie walked the grounds of George Washington's home hand in hand, pausing somberly at the first president's tomb and thinking of him striding the very same land.

Congress adjourned on March 4, and the next day Edward traveled with his daughters to Philadelphia. Old Amherst friends, the Colemans, now lived there, and their daughter Eliza was eager to see Emily and Vinnie again. Edward saw them safely to the Colemans' home and continued on to Amherst. The girls stayed with the Colemans for two weeks. During their visit they attended the Arch Street Presbyterian Church with the family. The church's minister, the Reverend Charles Wadsworth, was widely known for his remarkable sermons. Charles had been a poet before he became a minister and spoke eloquently and boldly, using beautiful imagery. Occasionally he surprised his listeners with a mischievous humor. One listener remarked that "his congregations were shaken as if by a whirlwind."

Emily, who could be moved by a powerful sermon, found Charles a magnetic presence who expressed the spiritual power and struggles she sometimes felt. His sly humor resembled her own. While her only experience of him during that Philadelphia visit was hearing his sermon, she came to consider him an important spiritual advisor. They met face-to-face just a few times, first in October 1859, but Wadsworth became one of the most significant figures in Emily's adult life.

Another important adult friendship was that of Dr. Josiah G. Holland and his wife, Elizabeth. Josiah was the literary editor of the *Springfield Daily Republican*. He and Elizabeth had attended Amherst Commencements since he began working at the newspaper in 1849 and had become acquainted with Edward. When they came to town for the July 1853 Commencement, they accepted an invitation to dine with the Dickinsons. Emily and the couple took a fancy to each other over champagne. The Hollands invited her and Vinnie to visit them in Springfield. The sisters happily accepted. They were guests in the Holland household in September 1853 and had such a good time that they returned again the following September.

Eager as she was to visit the Hollands a second time, Emily turned down her old friend Abiah Root's invitation, which came during the summer of 1854, when Sue was still suffering from a "nervous fever." Emily and Abiah had not been in frequent contact over the past few years, and Emily delayed for more than a month in replying. When she did, she expressed her reluctance to leave home (falsely, as we know, given her plans to visit the Hollands): "I dont go from home, unless emergency leads me by the hand, and then I do it obstinately, and draw back if I can. . . . My warmest thanks are your's, but dont expect me. I'm so old fashioned, Darling, that all your friends would stare." It was the last letter she wrote to her childhood friend.

In November 1855 the Homestead was at last ready for the Dickinsons. The move was difficult for both Emily and her mother. Even though she had been born there, Emily had left the Homestead at age nine. It was the house on West Street, where she had lived for nearly 15 years, with its pine grove, its orchard, and its gardens, that was home for Emily.

In mid-October, shortly before the move, Emily made sure, as she always did when the cold weather approached, to protect her plants from the frost. She walked for a last time through the gardens she had tended for so long. Admiring autumn's nuts, squirrels, and gold and scarlet trees, her cheeks ruddy and cold, she covered the plants as tenderly as though she were tucking bedclothes over her children.

Moving to the Homestead threw Emily into a chaotic state. She felt as though she had lost part of herself. For her mother it was worse. Soon after they moved in, she became an invalid, able only to lie on a couch or sit in an easy chair. She stayed in this condition for more than two years. Emily and Vinnie became both housekeepers and their mother's caretakers. Emily continued to love baking—in 1856 her round loaf of Indian and rye bread won second prize at the Amherst Cattle Show, and the following year she was asked to be one of the judges. But other forms of housework never appealed to her, and she found the increased housekeeping a burden. Being in a new house that was unfamiliar to both sisters made things even more difficult. They were glad when Margaret O'Brien came to work for the family as domestic help. While there was still plenty for Emily and Vinnie to do, Margaret became an indispensable part of the family for nine years.

Right around the time of the move, Emily's only family ally in the religious battle went over to the other side. One afternoon in church, listening to the sermon, Austin found himself, to his surprise, struck by the words "choose now." The words seemed to speak to him personally. A few weeks later, in church, he stood up and confessed his newly found belief in Christ. He became a full member of the church on January 6, 1856.

Sue, who had been trying to persuade Austin to accept Christ, even giving him books to read, was delighted. But Emily felt betrayed by her brother. And she felt very alone.

It wasn't that Emily didn't believe in God. The many poems she wrote about God, death, heaven, and the soul reflect a deep faith in the life of the spirit. And she listened thoughtfully to sermons at church, when she went, especially to those that were about wrestling with belief in God. But she didn't agree that people were born sinful and could not become good without God's help. Instead, she increasingly saw God's goodness and love everywhere around her, in the beauty of the world and the love of her family and dear friends. It was hard for her, though, to hold onto this faith when everyone around her, those very same people she loved, believed differently.

Emily believed that the nature of God and the after-life could only be a mystery to human beings. She wrote her friend Elizabeth Holland that "My only sketch, pro-file, of Heaven is a large, blue sky, bluer and larger than the *biggest* I have seen in June, and in it are my friends . . . those who are with me now, and those who were 'parted' as we walked, and 'snatched up to Heaven.'"

In the summer of 1856, Sue and Austin traveled to Sue's aunt in Geneva, New York, to be married. None of the Dickinsons attended the July 1 wedding, probably because of the mother's invalid condition. When the couple returned to Amherst, their new home was ready for them. They named it the Evergreens, after the pine grove that Austin had planted at the previous house.

One of the greatest religious revivals of all swept through the United States in the winter and spring of 1856–1857. All over the country, impassioned people swarmed into churches to confess their faith in Christ. In Philadelphia, Charles Wadsworth said the revival was only the third time in the history of Christianity that so many people converted. The era came to be known as the Great Awakening. In Amherst, Emily's First Congregational Church accepted 24 new members. It was an especially difficult season for Emily.

She turned more and more often to her writing—poems, for the most part, instead of the correspondence that had always taken so much of her time. It's difficult to know how many poems she wrote before 1858; only four have been found—the two published valentines, a short poem dated to 1853, and the one to Sue in 1854. But in 1858 she wrote—or copied over—at least 42 poems. Emily didn't put dates on her poems, but her handwriting changed from year to year. Those who knew her and her penmanship well, including Sue, were among the first to try to date her poems after her death, using her changing handwriting as clues. While it's unknown when she actually composed the original poems, her handwriting does reveal when she copied them into the versions found after her death.

During 1858, Emily began a secret project. She told nobody about it, not even Vinnie or Sue or Austin. She started to make little booklets of her poetry. She would copy what she considered the best drafts onto sheets of pre-folded stationery. When she put more than one poem on a page, she separated them with a long horizontal line. Then she stacked several sheets of paper together and, with a needle, made two holes in the left side of the folded papers. Using string—sometimes white, sometimes red-and-white, sometimes blue-and-white—she bound the papers together into a pocket-sized booklet.

Then she destroyed the earlier versions of the poems. Sometimes she also sent a copy of a poem to Sue or to other friends. But the booklets were Emily's secret. After she died, Vinnie discovered them. They have become known as Emily's fascicles, a word used to describe separately published installments of a book.

One of the poems she sent to Sue that year expresses the close feelings she continued to have for the friend who had become part of her own family. In the poem, Emily compares her "sister" Sue to Vinnie, the sister "in the house":

> One Sister have I in the house -
> And one a hedge away.
> There's only one recorded -
> But both belong to me.
>
> One came the road that I came -
> And wore my last year's gown -
> The other, as a bird her nest
> Builded our hearts among.

She did not sing as we did -
It was a different tune -
Herself to her a music
As Bumble bee of June.

Today is far from childhood,
But up and down the hills,
I held her hand the tighter -
Which shortened all the miles -

And still her hum
The years among,
Deceives the Butterfly;
And in her Eye
The Violets lie,
Mouldered this many May -

I spilt the dew,
But took the morn -
I chose this single star
From out the wide night's numbers -
Sue - forevermore!

It was wonderful for Emily to have Sue nearby, just "a hedge away." In addition to being part of Emily's daily life, Sue and Austin loved to entertain. The Evergreens was always filled with guests, and Emily was often among them. The house quickly became the center of Amherst's cultural life, and important visitors to the town, like Ralph Waldo Emerson, were commonly

Austin and Sue's home, the Evergreens.

invited to the Evergreens. At Sue and Austin's gatherings Emily thrived on a constant source of intellectual
and literary stimulation. She sometimes stayed so late
into the evening that Edward, worried as always, would
come over to take her home.

Emily made several close friends at the Evergreens.
One of the most important was Samuel Bowles, owner
and editor in chief of the *Springfield Daily Republican*. He
and his wife, Mary, first came to Amherst at the end of
June 1858 for an agricultural competition. Samuel was
interested in many things including literature, art, and
politics. He wasn't afraid to publish unpopular ideas if
he thought they were significant. Under his direction,

his newspaper had become an important publication. He traveled frequently and had much influence in Massachusetts and Washington, DC.

Samuel and Austin quickly became friends, and Emily, too, was drawn to his lively mind and daring manner. Very soon after the Bowleses left Amherst, she wrote to them, beginning, "I am sorry you came, because you went away. . . . I would like to have you dwell here."

She began to send some of her poems to Samuel, respecting his opinions on her work. She wasn't sending them for publication, but somehow, without her knowledge, one of her poems appeared in the *Springfield Daily Republican* just a few months after the Bowleses' first visit to Amherst. It was printed with no byline, and with a note acknowledging that the poem had been secretly obtained.

It was headed: "To Mrs. _____, with a Rose. [Surreptitiously communicated to the Republican.]"

Nobody knows this little Rose -
It might a pilgrim be
Did I not take it from the ways
And lift it up to thee.
Only a Bee will miss it -
Only a Butterfly,
Hastening from far journey -
On it's breast to lie -
Only a Bird will wonder -
Only a Breeze will sigh -

Ah Little Rose - how easy
For such as thee to die!

Sometime in 1858, probably in the early spring, before
she met Samuel and Mary Bowles, Emily composed a
mysterious letter. Written in ink on fine cream-colored,
blue-ruled stationery in lovely handwriting, it was
addressed "Dear Master" and begins with the declaration, "I am ill, but grieving more that you are ill, I make
my stronger hand work long eno' to tell you." Emily
seemed to be writing to somebody she feared had died,
because she went on to say, "I thought perhaps you were
in Heaven, and when you spoke again, it seemed quite
sweet, and wonderful, and surprised me so—I wish that
you were well." Her letter also sounds as though she
were answering somebody ("when you spoke again")
who had written to her. Emily made a few corrections
on it, then folded it into quarters, possibly for privacy.

To this day, nobody knows for sure who the letter was
to, or if she ever sent a different draft of it. One guess is that
it was to Charles Wadsworth, whose sermon in Philadelphia had so moved her. Some people even think it might
just have been a writing exercise, not meant for anybody
at all. Others guess that Emily might have been writing to
some secret part of herself that was troubling her.

This undated letter was the first of three she would
write addressed to the unknown Master. Of all the mysteries about Emily's life, the mystery of the Master is the
greatest.

10

THE POET IN FULL BLOOM

The illness Emily mentioned in her letter to the Master was just one of the troubles facing the family in the late 1850s. Emily and Vinnie were afraid to leave the house because their mother was still incapable of moving about. In late October 1858, Austin fell ill with typhoid fever, which made the entire family terribly anxious. Just days later, their stableman's eight-year-old daughter, Harriet, died of scarlet fever. Emily felt the presence of death everywhere. "I can't stay any longer in a world of death," she wrote Elizabeth Holland, mentioning Harriet and adding, "I buried my garden yesterday" and that "the woods are dead." Winter was coming and, as usual, Emily feared for her plants and mourned the bare trees.

Early in 1859, Aunt Lavinia came down with consumption. Vinnie went quickly to Boston to tend to her,
as Lavinia's daughters, Loo and Fanny, were just teen-
agers. When Edward made a trip to New York, Emily
was left alone with her mother. Emily was relying on
Vinnie more and more in many ways, and Vinnie's long
absence made her uneasy. She wrote a friend, "I feel the
oddest fright at parting with her for an hour, lest a storm
arise, and I go unsheltered." Emily was growing reluctant to visit neighbors by herself and sometimes even
excused herself from a social evening at the Evergreens
while Vinnie was away.

That year Emily was greatly taken by a new book.
Elizabeth Barrett Browning, whose poems meant so
much to her, had published a novel in verse entitled
Aurora Leigh just a few years earlier. By the time Emily
had a copy, it had already gathered much attention.
Samuel Bowles, who championed women writers, was
among the book's great admirers. *Aurora Leigh* explores
the importance of art and women artists. The story of a
young woman who initially turns down marriage for a
writing career, it describes the difficulties a woman faces
in her growth as a writer. Emily and Sue each had their
own copy of the book and marked the passages that were
especially meaningful to them. For Emily, it was both
illuminating and reassuring to read about a woman who
was able to become an important literary figure.

Emily's 29th birthday came in the midst of a five-day
storm—snow that turned to rain and then to fog. Austin

and Sue had gone to Boston, where Vinnie was again taking care of sick Aunt Lavinia, and Emily had only her dog, Carlo, for company. But she was cheered by a bright bouquet from Mary Bowles that included verbena and yellow heliotrope. Emily planted the heliotrope in her conservatory garden.

Vinnie came home for Christmas, but by March Aunt Lavinia was again doing so poorly that Vinnie had to return to Boston. She was there when Aunt Lavinia died on April 17. Emily was terribly shaken by the news; she had just sent her aunt a small bouquet of flowers and had baked a loaf of bread to send, too. She couldn't believe that while she had been baking, her aunt had been dying. Emily had lost many friends to death by now, but Aunt Lavinia was the first close family member.

Vinnie stayed on with Fanny, Loo, and their father for a little while after Aunt Lavinia's death. Emily corresponded with them more regularly than before. Now that they were 18 and 13 years old and had a shared loss and grief, she felt even closer to them. "Dear cousins," she wrote, "I know you both better than I did, and love you both better, and always I have a chair for you in the smallest parlor in the world, to wit, my heart." She also sent a poem of comfort:

> "Mama" never forgets her birds -
> Though in another tree.
> She looks down just as often
> And just as tenderly,

As when her little mortal nest
With cunning care she wove -
If either of her "sparrows fall",
She "notices" above.

After so much death, the birth of Sue and Austin's first child in June 1861 should have been an occasion for celebration. Instead, his birth was especially poignant for two reasons. He arrived on a sad anniversary: exactly 11 years to the day after Sue's sister Mary had given birth to her own first child and died soon after. And then, just five days earlier, sister Martha, now married and living in Geneva, New York, had lost her first baby. Neither Sue nor the baby suffered from the birth, which was an enormous relief to all. But the baby was sickly for many months, and until December he had no official name. He was called simply Jacky.

In December, Sue wrote on behalf of her little boy to Edward, asking if he might have the same name as his grandfather. Edward replied, characteristically, "If you will be a good boy, ride in your carriage & not cry, and always mind your father and mother, I will consent to your being called Edward Dickinson." The baby was named Edward and known as Ned.

For Emily, Ned's birth was as much a shock as it was a delight. She loved children, in general, but she had little experience interacting with an actual infant. And suddenly she had to share Sue with not only Austin but also her nephew. Not being a mother herself, it was hard for her to imagine how all-consuming it could be to care for a child. And even though Sue had a nurse to help her, now that she was a mother she could never devote her attention to Emily the way she once had—and the way Emily so deeply wanted her to. She was used to sharing many of her poems with Sue and receiving Sue's thoughtful critiques. Now she felt very alone. The death

Austin and Sue's first child, Ned, age 17.

of her beloved Elizabeth Barrett Browning the same month as Ned's birth was also upsetting.

Suffering with the many recent sorrows, she turned again, sometime in 1861—probably in the spring—to the mysterious Master. Referring to herself as "Daisy" (a flower she identified with because it was so common) she writes with desperate apology for some unspecified offense, and of anguished love. She talks about having a "cough as big as a thimble" and a "Tomahawk in my side but that dont hurt me much." Only her Master's stab wounds her.

In the letter, she describes "A love so big it scares her, rushing among her small heart" and begs her Master to "open your life wide, and take me in forever." She promises to be "your best little girl."

Compared to the letter of 1858, this one is a wildly rough draft. It's written in pencil, in almost careless handwriting, with many corrections. This letter is folded only in half. Strangely, Emily used incredibly luxurious—cream-colored and gilt-edged—stationery for this emotional and anguished draft. We will never know if it was copied over and actually sent to somebody. The intensity of feeling it expresses is echoed in a poem written that year that hints at her longing for a hidden love:

> Wild nights - Wild nights!
> Were I with thee
> Wild nights should be
> Our luxury!

Futile - the winds -
To a Heart in port -
Done with the Compass -
Done with the Chart!

Rowing in Eden -
Ah - the Sea!
Might I but moor - tonight -
In thee!

To Emily's surprise, one of her poems appeared in the May 4 edition of the *Springfield Daily Republican*. Like the poem published in August 1858, it appeared anonymously. Titled "The May Wine," the poem is one of Emily's more well known. It begins: "I taste a liquor never brewed - / From Tankards scooped in Pearl - / Not all the Frankfort Berries / Yield such an Alcohol!" While Emily continued to send her poems to Samuel Bowles, she did so because she relied on his personal criticism. She didn't expect him to publish them or even to consider them for publication. Again, it's unclear how this poem found its way into the newspaper.

By this time, the newspapers were full of the Civil War, which had begun in April 1861. Amherst, while far from the action, was filled with talk of the war from its beginning. A total of 273 men from the town enlisted over the years, and many were killed or wounded. Emily wrote with distress to Cousin Loo after Christmas 1861 about a local boy who had died from a wound in Annapolis. His death was especially awful for the town because his brother had died from a fever just a few months before. And now the president of Amherst College was visiting his enlisted son, Frazer Stearns, in Annapolis. "I hope that ruddy face won't be brought home frozen," Emily lamented to Loo.

Sadly, only a few months later, in March 1862, Frazer Stearns was killed in battle. His body returned to Amherst in a large closed casket covered with flowers. Crowds of townspeople, including Emily, came to honor and mourn him. Austin was especially shaken. He could not stop repeating "Frazer is killed, Frazer is killed."

During the early 1860s Emily wrote more poetry than at any other time of her life. In 1862 she wrote 226 poems, including some of her best-known. She had written to Samuel Bowles in 1858 that "My friends are my 'estate.' Forgive me then the avarice to hoard them!"; but one of her 1862 poems seems to describe her increasing desire to limit her friends and retreat from others: "The Soul selects her own Society - / Then - shuts the Door - ."

A short verse reflects on the power of language: "A word is dead, when it is said / Some say - / I say it just begins to live / That day." Another of her most famous poems, also written in 1862, is often quoted for comfort:

> "Hope" is the thing with feathers -
> That perches in the soul -
> And sings the tune without the words -
> And never stops - at all -

And sweetest - in the Gale - is heard -
And sore must be the storm -
That could abash the little Bird
That kept so many warm -

I've heard it in the chillest land -
And on the strangest Sea -
Yet - never - in Extremity,
It asked a crumb - of me.

In April 1862 an article in the *Atlantic Monthly*, a leading intellectual magazine of the time (which is still published today), caught Emily's attention. Entitled "Letter to a Young Contributor" and written by Thomas Wentworth Higginson, the article was directed to beginning writers. Emily, now intensely engaged in writing poetry, was

Thomas Wentworth
Higginson.

enthralled by the advice and encouragement offered in the article. She wrote to Thomas, enclosing four of her poems and asking for his opinion. This letter was the beginning of a correspondence that lasted until Emily died. Although they met only twice, Thomas became one of her most important friends.

It was to Thomas, as well as to Samuel Bowles, that Emily sent much of her poetry. She looked to the two of them for thoughtful feedback. Thomas was a minister, a devoted abolitionist (abolitionists were fierce opponents of slavery), and, like Samuel, a strong supporter of women's rights. Like Emily, he loved nature, and had published essays about New England's natural life. So it's not surprising that Emily decided to risk entrusting her very precious work to his critique. She asked him in her first letter if her "Verse is alive?" She wrote with humility and gratitude for his attention.

Thomas found the four poems Emily sent him promising enough to comment upon and encouraged her with questions. When she received his reply, along with edited versions of her poems, she was sick in bed and could not answer for several days. When she did, she thanked him for what she called his "surgery" on her work and told him "it was not so painful as I supposed." She enclosed more poems with the second letter.

In this second letter she told him about the poets she enjoyed (John Keats, Elizabeth Barrett Browning, and her husband, Robert Browning), other books that were meaningful to her—including the Bible—and about the other "Tutors" she had had, referring without name to Benjamin Franklin Newton and Samuel Bowles. Her best companions, she noted, were the hills, sundown, and her big dog. As to her family, she described them as religious, except for herself, and expressed the honor she felt when she read Thomas's work in the *Atlantic*. She also confided that she had been living in "a terror" since September, a secret terror that she could only express through her poetry.

This terror might have had something to do with the emotions she expressed in a third letter to her Master, most likely written in the summer of 1861. This letter is also composed in beautiful handwriting, in ink (with revisions in both pencil and ink), on two sheets of cream-colored stationery, embossed with a queen's head. Emily folded it into thirds.

Again, Emily refers to herself occasionally as "Daisy" and describes her longing for her Master's presence. She asks: "Could'nt Carlo, and you and I walk in the meadows an hour - and nobody care but the Bobolink - ?" She writes that she wanted to die sooner so that she could be with him in heaven. "I want to see you more - Sir - than all I wish for in this world. . . . Could you come to New England . . . would you come to Amherst - Would you like to come - Master?" This invitation gives the clue that her Master is somebody who lives outside of New England.

This is the last letter to the mysterious Master. Even though there are only three—a tiny number compared to Emily's extensive other correspondences—the Master letters have continued to mystify and intrigue Dickinson scholars ever since their discovery. Emily was clearly successful at keeping the secrets that were most important to her.

Far less mysterious is Emily's correspondence with Thomas Higginson. (Though a few scholars have suspected him of being the Master, this idea has been widely debunked due to the tone of their known correspondence.) Early on, Thomas described Emily's work as "spasmodic" and "uncontrolled." He advised her to delay publishing, and she smiled at the idea. Publishing, she wrote him, was not in her plans. She had no interest in fame, she told him. She wanted to develop her writing and asked for his continued guidance.

As summer came on with its roses, honeysuckles, morning glory, and robins, Loo and Fanny came from Boston for the annual Commencement activities that were always such a big event for the Dickinson family. Samuel Bowles, who usually attended and reported on the event for the *Springfield Daily Republican*, was traveling in Europe. Emily asked him, if he were to visit Elizabeth Barrett Browning's grave in Florence, Italy, to please place his hand on the gravestone on Emily's behalf.

That November when Samuel returned from his many months in Europe, one of his first visits was to the Dickinson home. Much to his astonishment, Emily refused to see him. She sent a brief note downstairs for him, writing that she was thrilled at his return, and to hear his voice below, but that she could not see him. Was this the start of Emily's need for seclusion, even from some of her dearest friends? When Vinnie and Austin reprimanded her for her behavior, she explained that she simply wanted them to enjoy Samuel's company without her interference. The explanation did not satisfy anybody.

When the new year came, tragedy struck Emily's young cousins again. In January 1863, Loo and Fanny lost their father. Emily sent them a poem, saying "Let Emily sing for you because she cannot pray." In February she tried to cheer them with letters describing the beautiful flowers growing in her conservatory in the midst of winter: crocuses, primroses, heliotropes, sweet asylum, and a fuchsia (which the cat, Emily noted, tried to eat, mistaking it for strawberries!).

Now Loo and Fanny were orphans. To make matters worse, their father's death left them without the means to keep up their home. They stayed with the Dickinsons for a while in the early autumn and took comfort in being with the family. Sometimes Loo sat outside the kitchen pantry on a foot stool, listening to Emily recite the poetry she was composing as she skimmed the milk. When the girls left Amherst, they gave up their home and moved into a boardinghouse in Cambridge, near Boston.

Emily wrote more poems in 1863 than any other year of her life—nearly 300. But before the year was over, she started to have trouble with her eyes. All of the Dickinsons suffered from eye trouble, but Emily's was worse than Vinnie's or Austin's. Her eyes hurt more and more, especially when she looked at bright lights. By February 1864 she was suffering so much that she went to Boston to consult with a renowned ophthalmologist (eye doctor), Dr. Henry Willard Williams. Dr. Williams was a reassuring and gentle man, and after examining Emily he was confident that a series of his treatments could help her.

So in late April 1864, Emily moved into the Cambridge boardinghouse with Loo and Fanny. Until November she lived with her cousins and underwent Dr. Williams's treatments in nearby Boston. The treatments were painful, and worst of all for Emily, the doctor didn't want her to write letters—or poems, of course. She defied him as much as she could, writing short notes to Sue and Vinnie, whom she missed terribly. When her nephew Ned's third birthday came, she managed a funny little letter to him, as well. The doctor had taken away her pen, so she wrote in pencil. Lou and Fanny cared for her, and she was very grateful, but she never got used to being away from her home, her family, and Carlo.

As Thanksgiving approached, the doctor finally decided Emily was ready to go home. She asked Vinnie to come alone to meet her train. On November 21 Emily joyously returned to Amherst. She spent her first weeks reacquainting herself with her beloved plants. She cooked, baked, and knitted. But her eyes continued to ache, and her family noticed.

By early 1865, Emily realized she would have to return to Dr. Williams for more treatments. She dreaded the idea of leaving home again. But she had written fewer than 100 poems in 1864, and she knew she could not continue to write as long as her eyes caused her so much trouble. As the new year began, Emily prepared for yet another absence from her beloved home.

SHUNNING SOCIETY, SEEKING SECLUSION

I n April 1865 Emily left for Boston, just as she had
the previous April. For six months she stayed again
with Loo and Fanny in their Cambridge boardinghouse
while undergoing treatments with Dr. Williams. Spring
in Boston was hot and rainy; mosquitoes buzzed around
as though it were August instead of May. As during her
earlier treatments, she was forbidden from writing or
reading, but she managed short notes to Sue and Vinnie.

This series of treatments was more successful than
the first. After Emily returned home, she never again
complained of eye trouble. She was happy to get back to
her family but sad to learn that their longtime servant,
Margaret O'Brien, was leaving to get married. The Dickinson women had always worked alongside their help at

the household chores. Emily and Margaret used to clean up the dishes together; Emily would wash and Margaret would dry. The family missed Margaret so much that they didn't replace her for nearly four years. With no servant, more and more housework fell to Emily and Vinnie.

Throughout the late 1860s, Thomas Higginson remained one of Emily's regular correspondents, and she often enclosed a few poems for his critique in her letters. Thomas grew eager to meet Emily and invited her to Boston several times. Each time she refused, first explaining that her father did not like her to leave home. "He is in the habit of me," she wrote Higginson.

Edward was especially "in the habit of" Emily's baking. He would only eat bread that she baked. He also loved the desserts she made; Emily's gingerbread and "black cake" (which took five pounds of raisins, as well as cloves, nutmeg, and cinnamon) were always huge successes. Friends like Sue and Elizabeth Holland begged for the recipes, and Emily graciously shared them. (Even after a new servant, Maggie, arrived in 1869, Edward still insisted on Emily's bread and desserts.)

In January 1866 Emily lost one of her closest companions when her dog, Carlo, died. He had stayed by her side for nearly 20 years. Carlo had meant so much to Emily that she never got another dog. It was only a small comfort when her conservatory bloomed that winter with exotic flowers that made her think of Indonesia's Spice Islands.

A few months after Carlo's death, little Ned was sick for a week, which made the whole family nervous. When he was finally back on his rocking horse (though still pale and ghostly looking) Emily wrote happily to Elizabeth Holland. "He inherits his Uncle Emily's ardor for the lie," she bragged, when he said that "the Clock purrs and the Kitten ticks." (She occasionally referred to herself mischievously as "Uncle.") By spring, everybody was encouraged to see Ned back to playing as usual, chasing imaginary animals with a long stick and visiting daily with the real hens and horses in the barn.

The week of Valentine's Day in 1866, Emily's poem "The Snake" appeared in the *Springfield Daily Republican*. Again, there was the mystery of who had sent it to the newspaper. Emily was not happy for several reasons. First of all, she didn't like seeing her work published. Secondly, a question mark had been inserted at the end of the third line, which she felt changed the meaning and rhythm. She had written, "A narrow Fellow in the Grass / Occasionally rides - / You may have met Him - did you not / His notice sudden is."

The version in the newspaper read: "A narrow Fellow in the Grass / Occasionally rides - / You may have met him - did you not? His notice instant is." With the question mark after "not," a question was being asked that she did not mean to ask. She was writing about the surprise of suddenly sighting a snake in the grass.

She wrote to Thomas with some embarrassment— after all, she had told him she wasn't interested in publication and here was her poem in the newspaper. Even though it was published anonymously, she knew he would recognize it since she had sent him a copy. She told him she had been "robbed" of the poem and "defeated" by the change in the third line. This letter is the only record that exists of Emily ever commenting on the publication of one of her poems without her permission. There was some suspicion that it was Sue who had sent the poem to the paper. Samuel Bowles was a great friend of hers and Austin's, and Emily often shared her poems with her sister-in-law.

In November 1866 the Dickinson family grew with the birth of Sue and Austin's second child, a little girl they named Martha, after Sue's sister. Everyone called her Mattie. Now Sue had two children to care for. Meanwhile Emily was growing more and more reluctant to walk the path from the Homestead to the Evergreens. Her and Sue's relationship was still deeply important to her—she continued to ask for Sue's opinion on her poems and continued an intimate correspondence with her—but she saw her sister-in-law less and less.

Thomas Higginson continued to invite Emily to Boston, and she continued to refuse. With her third refusal, she admitted that "I do not cross my Father's ground to any House or town." She invited him to come to Amherst instead. She told him he probably didn't realize he had "saved her life" and that she wanted more than anything to thank him in person. Thomas tried to lure Emily with promises of interesting literary meetings at

Martha "Mattie" Dickinson, Austin and Susan's daughter, age three.

a friend's home or a music festival in the city. But when he and Emily finally met face-to-face, in August 1870, it was at the Homestead.

Their meeting, after all the years of intense corre-spondence, was momentous for both. Waiting for Emily, Thomas heard what sounded like a child's footsteps. Then Emily entered the room, wearing a white dress and a light blue shawl. She carried two daylilies, which she offered to Thomas in introduction. Her voice was soft, childlike, and a little frightened. She apologized for being afraid, explaining that she never saw strangers and didn't know what to say.

In spite of her initial fright, she quickly began to talk, stopping occasionally to invite him to speak but then spilling forth her thoughts again. She told him about her love of reading, how Edward had insisted they read only the Bible when they were young and how she and Austin had to sneak novels into the house. She told him how much Shakespeare meant to her. She offered him her definition of poetry: "If I read a book [and] it makes my whole body so cold no fire ever can warm me I know *that* is poetry. If I feel physically as if the top of my head were taken off, I know *that* is poetry."

After an hour with Emily, Thomas was exhausted—though fascinated. He wrote to his wife that evening, describing the visit and guessing that she would have found some of Emily's talk foolish, but that he found much of it wise. Still, he was afraid to question Emily directly when he didn't understand something she said. He had a feeling that a direct question would make her withdraw from him. As for Emily, she felt that Thomas "ask[ed] great questions accidentally." Being with him in person instead of reading his words on paper was at once unreal and unbearably sweet.

Before leaving Amherst the next day, Thomas returned to the Homestead. His second conversation

with Emily was equally fascinating and equally drain-
ing. He found her remarks so intriguing that, afterward,
he made it a point to write down everything he could
remember. And although it seemed to Thomas that she
lived a strange life, he noted that she found it joyful, saying, "I find ecstasy in living—the mere sense of living is
joy enough."

After the second visit, Thomas wrote again to his
wife, saying he had enjoyed his time with Emily very
much. While he found her considerate of other people,
he added that he had never been with anybody who
took so much out of him. In spite of his fascination with
Emily, he concluded, he was glad that he lived a good
distance away. (Not until December 1873 did he make a
second, and last, visit to her.)

By the time of Higginson's visit, Emily had stopped
going to the Evergreens altogether. Her relationship
with Sue remained vital, though; the two communicated regularly through letters, and Emily still sent her
poems to her dear friend. Austin, on the other hand,
was at the Homestead more than ever, sometimes stopping in several times a day. His and Sue's marriage had
stopped making either of them happy some time ago.
His close relationships with his parents and sisters, as
well as his deep involvement in the growth of the town
of Amherst, seemed to be more important to him than
spending time with his wife.

Emily had stopped copying poems into fascicles in
1864. By the late 1870s, she was using whatever scraps

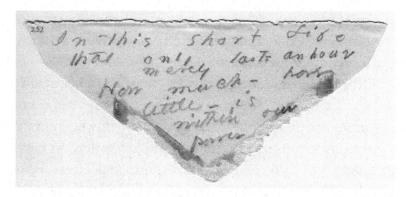

Beginning in the late 1870s, Emily wrote her poems on whatever scraps of paper she could find, including used envelopes.
This one, Poem 1292, written on an envelope flap, reads: "In
this short life that only lasts an hour / How much - how little - is within our power." She also wrote the word "merely"
below "only," as if she hadn't yet made up her mind which
word to use.

of paper she could find—envelopes, wrapping paper,
Commencement programs—to draft her poems. Her
handwriting was tiny, so entire poems fit on the oddly
shaped scraps she collected for this purpose. She wrote
more and more often in pencil, not pen, and usually carried a small pencil nub along with a few scraps of paper
in a right-hand pocket of her dress.

It was unusual for her to make a clean copy of a
poem. If she did, it was often to enclose the poem in
a letter to a friend. Frequent recipients of her poems
included Sue, Thomas Higginson, Elizabeth Holland,
Samuel Bowles, and cousins Loo and Fanny, with whom
she corresponded very often about details of daily life

at the Homestead. Most years Loo and Fanny came to the Amherst College Commencement activities, a visit Emily always looked forward to.

Otherwise, though, she saw less and less of her neighbors and friends in the community. She preferred writing notes, often accompanied by a single flower stem or a carefully arranged bouquet from her garden, to congratulate or console people. These notes and letters were usually affectionate and witty; some read like poems themselves. Through her correspondence, Emily stayed involved in Amherst goings-on and her friends' lives.

She also kept informed by eavesdropping. When visitors came to the Homestead, Emily liked to stand in the upstairs hallway (sometimes with little Mattie at her side), so she could overhear their conversations. Even when her old friend Abby Wood, now Mrs. Bliss and a missionary in Syria, came to Amherst in 1873, Emily refused to see her at first. Abby insisted, though, and Emily finally relented. Abby was distressed to see how Emily had aged and told her so. She tried to encourage her to resume the more active social life she remembered enjoying with Emily.

For Emily, though, the small talk and niceties that social life involved were becoming too difficult. Her complicated thoughts and deep emotions filled her and overflowed into letters and poems. She took care of her beloved gardens only when she could be sure nobody was nearby. One of her favorite times for gardening was in the very early morning.

In November 1873, when he was almost 71 years old, Edward was drawn back into politics. He was elected to the Massachusetts House of Representatives. Reluctant to leave home and busy with Amherst town affairs as well as his legal practice, he nevertheless felt the strong obligation to serve. In January 1874, a few days after his 71st birthday, he rented rooms in a Boston boarding-house not far from where the legislature met daily. The work was exhausting, and Edward soon felt run-down.

In mid-June there was a short recess, and Edward returned to Amherst on a Thursday. He was due back in Boston on Monday morning and spent most of Sunday afternoon quietly with Emily. Vinnie was napping and Emily, feeling a sudden yearning to have her father to herself, made an excuse for her mother to be absent. By now Emily's family was used to her being often alone, so Edward was happy to spend this time with his daugh-ter. At the end of the afternoon he commented that he "would like it to not end." Emily was almost embar-rassed by his pleasure in her company.

Monday morning Emily woke Edward in time for him to catch an early train to Boston. The next evening she, Vinnie, and their mother were eating supper when Austin arrived with a telegram in his hand. Emily could tell by the look on his face that he had bad news.

Their father had suddenly fallen very ill, Austin told them. He was leaving for Boston right away and wanted Vinnie to come with him. The last train for the day had already left, so he had ordered their horses to be prepared for the journey. Before the horses were ready, though, a second message arrived. Edward had died.

Emily was so overcome by grief that she couldn't even attend the simple funeral held at the house three days later. She closed herself in her bedroom, crying uncontrollably, while Vinnie and the others mourned together. At the end of June, a memorial service was held at the First Congregational Church. Again, Emily couldn't bring herself to attend. Her grief at her father's death was so deep and lasted so long that she was never able to visit his grave. "Home is so far from Home, since my Father died," she wrote Thomas Higginson more than a year later. Even in her grief, she thought it right that her father's last day on earth with his family had been a Sunday, the dearest day of the week for him. It felt especially poignant to her that a card was found in her father's pocket when he died, reading (in his handwriting) "I hereby give myself to God."

Exactly one year after Edward's death, Emily's mother suffered a stroke. It left her with paralysis and memory loss. She didn't remember that her husband had died. She constantly asked Emily and Vinnie where he was and why he wasn't home yet. Many nights she begged Emily not to go to sleep until Edward arrived, so that somebody would be awake to greet him.

Vinnie and Emily now had the huge responsibility of caring for their mother in addition to running the household. Still, just a few months later, on August 1, Sue and Austin's third child was born, and Emily offered to send their servant Maggie to help.

Named Thomas Gilbert Dickinson, the baby was nicknamed Gib. The whole family, including Emily, soon came to adore him. Everybody attended the circuses he liked to organize in the Evergreens' yard. Even Ned, 14 years older, and Mattie, 8 years older, thought their little brother was very special. As he grew, Gib charmed everyone. Once he burst into the Homestead, saying, "Oh Aunt Emily, I want something."

"What shall it be?" Emily asked, giving him a kiss.

"Oh, everything," he answered.

Even though Emily kept to herself more and more, she enjoyed surprising her niece, nephews, and their playmates with treats. She liked hearing them play in the yard below her bedroom and never minded the noise they made as they played hide-and-seek or a game called "Gypsy and Pirate." Sometimes, in her own way, she joined in the game. In the middle of Gypsy and Pirate, for example, the children would suddenly receive a signal from the house. Then Emily, always keeping hidden, would slowly lower a basket on a rope from her bedroom window.

When the basket finally landed on the ground, the children—without interrupting the game—would slowly sneak over and take out some of Emily's famous gingerbread cakes. The children never knew if Emily lowered the basket so slowly to add suspense to the game or because she didn't want Maggie to notice she was giving gingerbread to the children. If Emily didn't have gingerbread, she secretly took cookies or doughnuts from the pantry to fill the basket, instead.

Of course, Ned, Mattie, Gib, and their friends adored Emily for sneaking treats to them and for being part of their games in this way. She sent them funny notes, too. One July day after Ned had been stung by a hornet, she wrote to him, "You know I never liked you in those Yellow Jackets." They loved it when she asked one of them to help her water the plants in her conservatory or help with her baking or deliver the notes she wrote to neighbors.

As much as she didn't enjoy being in the company of other adults (except her family, of course), Emily took pleasure in being part of the children's lives. Her life was full, with gardening, baking, correspondence, and, especially, poetry. But her heart was often heavy; more than three years after her father's death, Emily still mourned him. She still wrote about him in letters to friends. Whenever somebody died, she thought of her father. The death of the wife of one of Edward's closest friends, Otis Phillips Lord, in late 1877 was another reminder of her loss. When she learned of Elizabeth Lord's death, though, Emily had no idea of the effect it would have on her own life.

THE FINAL YEARS— LOVE, AND MUCH LOSS

For all of her life, Emily's friends were of the greatest importance to her. Other than possibly the mysterious Master, though, she does not seem to have experienced significant romantic love. In the later years of her life, that changed. Sometime following Elizabeth Lord's death, Emily and Otis Lord, 18 years her senior, developed a passionate romance. Unsurprisingly, it was conducted primarily through correspondence.

A longtime friend of the Dickinson family, Otis Phillips Lord was a highly respected judge on the Massachusetts Supreme Court. He had also been a prominent politician and a proud member of the Whig Party, like Edward, and had served as Speaker of the Massachusetts

House of Representatives. He had graduated from Amherst College in 1832 and often returned to the town from his home in Salem, where he lived with his wife, on the Massachusetts coast north of Boston.

The Lords visited often with the Dickinsons, and a warm friendship grew between the families. Like the rest of her family, Emily admired and enjoyed Otis's intelligent and compelling company. She and Vinnie both occasionally corresponded with him; Sue visited with the Lords at the seaside. After Edward's death, Emily felt a deep affection for the man who had been so close to her father. And it was meaningful to Emily that Otis had been geographically nearer to Edward at the time of his death than she had.

After Edward's death, Otis took special care to check on the Dickinsons. He and Elizabeth spent a week with the family, when he helped Emily and her mother make their wills. Sometime in 1877, when he learned that Emily and Austin had both been sick, Otis wrote Vinnie to ask about their health. He believed that Emily had, in a recent letter to him, hidden the true state of her health so as not to worry him. He mentioned his wife's poor state, attributing it to a few ordinary afflictions. Later that year, though, Otis's worry about his wife deepened. It turned out she was suffering from cancer. Elizabeth Lord died on December 10, 1877—Emily's 47th birthday.

In a letter that month to Elizabeth Holland, Emily remarked on the loss of Elizabeth Lord as one of several troubling occurrences. Samuel Bowles, seriously ill for some time, seemed to be hovering near death. Vinnie was making a slow recovery from a severe illness, which had their mother—still bedridden and suffering memory loss—in an even greater state of despair. Emily and Maggie had their hands full nursing the two of them.

It's not clear when Emily and Otis's romance began. It was certainly strong by the late 1870s; by then Emily was writing passionate love letters to him. (It's important to remember that the only correspondence that has been found are drafts Emily saved of her letters to Otis.) She called him "Sweet One" and "Naughty one" and rejoiced in her love for him. They wrote to each other every Sunday. Emily marked the days of the week by how soon she would hear from Otis. Tuesdays were depressing because she knew it was too soon for him to begin writing his next letter. She lived in a constant state of anticipation.

Otis Phillips Lord.

Their romance was probably in full bloom by August 1880, when Otis came to Amherst, along with his nieces, for a full week—a longer visit than he had ever made to the town. He returned less than a month later—the shortest time ever between visits. He brought Emily a lavish gift: a beautiful volume of Shakespeare's works.

Fervent as Emily and Otis's shared passion was, Emily did not neglect her friends or her poetry. She grieved when Samuel Bowles died in January 1878, writing thoughtful letters to his widow. She congratulated Thomas Higginson on his marriage in February 1879. (His first wife had died in 1877 after being ill much of her life.) And she pursued a new literary friendship with writer Helen Hunt Jackson, whom she met through Higginson. The friendship with Helen resulted in the publication of one of Emily's poems in an 1878 anthology entitled *A Masque of Poets*. Appearing anonymously, of course, the poem was one she had written nearly 20 years before; today it remains one of her best known:

> Success is counted sweetest
> By those who ne'er succeed.
> To comprehend a nectar
> Requires sorest need.
>
> Not one of all the purple Host
> Who took the Flag today
> Can tell the definition
> So clear of Victory

As he defeated - dying -
On whose forbidden ear
The distant strains of triumph
Burst agonized and clear!

It was Helen who convinced Emily to permit the publication of this poem. Coincidentally, Helen had spent her early years in Amherst, attending Amherst Academy at the same time as Emily, though much more briefly. Helen had spent most of her girlhood away at a succession of schools, and the two had not known each other very well. Now, though, Helen had learned of Emily's work through Thomas Higginson, and Emily had expressed admiration of Helen's published writings to their mutual friend, as well.

When Helen and her husband visited Amherst in October 1878, Emily shocked everybody by agreeing to meet them. Helen followed up the visit with notes pleading for permission to send "Success" in her own handwriting (because she knew it by heart) to the publisher of the upcoming anthology. When *A Masque of Poets* appeared, critics attributed Emily's anonymous poem as being "most probably" by Ralph Waldo Emerson.

In her later years, the writings of Charles Wadsworth, whose sermon had so inspired her when she heard him preach in Philadelphia in 1855, continued to be important to Emily. From that first experience, she had felt an affinity for Wadsworth's sermons and writings on spirituality and suffering, subjects so integral to her own mind and heart. The tone and subjects of his sermons and those of her poems are often similar.

Some scholars suspect that Charles may have been the Master she wrote to in the late 1850s. But Charles was married with children, and even if Emily was in love with him, there is no evidence that he felt the same. Romantic feelings aside, there is no doubt that Charles was an important guiding figure for Emily. After his death, she described him as her "closest earthly friend" and "my 'Heavenly Father.'"

So she was happily surprised one summer day in 1880, as she was tending to her lilies and heliotropes, to hear Vinnie say, "The Gentleman with the deep voice wants to see you, Emily." While Emily rarely saw anybody anymore, she leaped at the opportunity to spend some time with Charles. She had met him only once before, more than 20 years earlier, when he had come to Amherst after his mother's death. This time he had come on impulse, without advance notice. This was their second and final meeting; less than two years later, in April 1882, he died of pneumonia.

While so much of Emily's energy was consumed by her correspondence and her poems, she also devoted herself to her mother. By the time of Wadsworth's visit, it was clear that her mother would never walk again. Each morning, she had to be carried from her bed to a chair, and back again in the evening. She enjoyed occasional visits from the parson and from friends who stopped in. Daily, Emily read to her, fanned her, and reassured her that she would feel better the next day. Vinnie, meanwhile, tended to almost everything else in the household.

Austin continued to come often to the Homestead. Emily noted that they sometimes forgot he had ever married and moved into his own home. His and Sue's marriage continued to suffer, which Emily, Vinnie, and their mother knew. Still, they were surprised when Austin openly fell in love with a new Amherst resident, Mabel Loomis Todd. Mabel's husband, David Todd, had been appointed astronomy instructor and director of the Amherst College Observatory. The couple and their year-old child, Millicent, arrived in town in August 1881. A writer, painter, and musician, Mabel quickly took to life in Amherst. When she and Austin met, they quickly took to each other. They made no effort to hide their love from their families, and their romance continued until Austin's death in 1895.

Knowing how unhappy Austin was with Sue, Emily and Vinnie had mixed feelings about his love affair with Mabel. Vinnie supported Austin's unconventional behavior, wanting him to be happy no matter what. Emily was torn; she also cared deeply for Austin's happiness but felt a great loyalty to her dear friend Sue. And while Austin and Mabel tried to keep their romance from the general public, people did talk, which made things difficult for their families. The couple's love and devotion to each other created a great strain for the Todds and the Dickinsons.

In the spring of 1882 Emily's mother, though feeble and frail, was still hanging on to life, for which Emily expressed daily gratitude. Stricken by grief at Charles Wadsworth's death on April 1, Emily's spirits were lifted by a visit from Otis later that month. After he returned to Salem, he reported to her that he had a cold. She replied that she had been worried during his stay that he might be coming down with something. She went on to write of her love for him: "I do—do want you tenderly. The Air is soft as Italy, but when it touches me, I spurn it with a Sigh, because it is not you."

May 1, the day Emily finished this letter, Otis's cold turned into something much more severe, and he fell into unconsciousness. It was Vinnie who gave Emily the troubling news. Coming in after talking with Austin, Vinnie asked her sister, "Did you see anything in the Paper that concerned us?" Emily said she had not, and Vinnie gave her the news: "Mr Lord is very sick."

Emily nearly blacked out herself. Her vision started to slip away, a coldness came over her body, and she grabbed at a chair to keep from falling. At that moment, the Dickinsons' handyman, Tom Kelley, who often posted her letters to Otis, came into the room, and Emily ran to him. Burying her face in his blue jacket, she began to weep. Tom tried to comfort her: "He will be better. Dont cry, Miss Emily."

A neighbor came by and helped Emily send a telegram asking about Otis's current state. Her fear that he was dying—or already dead—lasted until the next day.

Austin brought her the morning newspaper, and they searched for news of him but found nothing. Emily was both relieved and disturbed. But later that day a note arrived from Otis's niece; the judge was improving. Emily was rapturous with joy. In time he recovered, and soon he and Emily continued their romantic correspondence.

Just six months later, Emily's mother died. Long as her illness had been, her death felt unexpected to the siblings. Emily wrote to a friend, "The dear Mother that could not walk, has *flown*. It never occurred to us that though she had not Limbs, she had *Wings*—and she soared from us as unexpectedly as a summoned Bird." While Emily and her mother had not been especially close throughout most of Emily's life, when her mother became an invalid their bond deepened. Her absence felt very strange and sad to Emily.

But with her mother's death came an exciting possibility: now that Emily was free from the responsibility of her mother's care, Otis Lord wanted to marry her. Emily considered the tempting idea, trying out the name Emily Lord, but ultimately decided against marriage. She was firmly rooted in Amherst and the life she had created for herself. Their relationship continued, however, through their correspondence.

The Dickinsons were still grieving for their mother when, the following June, Ned came down with acute rheumatic fever, a serious infectious disease. For weeks the family waited anxiously, praying for his recovery.

On his birthday, June 19, Emily sent him a poignant note: "Stay with us one more Birthday, Ned—'Yesterday, Today, and Forever,' then we will let you go."

Ned did recover, but within a few months tragedy struck the Dickinsons again. One early autumn day, eight-year-old Gib was playing in a mud hole with his friend Kendall Emerson. By the next day, he was too sick to go to school. He had picked up an infection in the mud hole. Within a few days he had developed typhoid fever.

Panic and alarm fell over both households. Austin and Sue tended to him day and night, but the fever was fierce. Over the following days, it became clear that Gib would not survive. The night he was dying, Emily, accompanied by Maggie, walked the path that led from the Homestead to the Evergreens to sit vigil by her beloved nephew. It was the first time in 15 years that she had entered Austin and Sue's house. The smell of the disinfectants was so strong she could barely tolerate it, but she stayed by the delirious boy's side.

"Open the Door, open the Door, they are waiting for me," Gib cried out once. Emily wondered who he saw waiting for him. Could it be his grandmother who, like everyone, had so loved his open heart, his lively nature, his sweet wit? (In a letter to Santa Claus, he had written "Please bring me whatever you think best. I don't mean a spanking I mean some common place toys.")

At about three in the morning, Emily felt so sick from the smell that she had to leave. When she returned to

Thomas Gilbert "Gib" Dickinson, Emily's nephew.

the Homestead, she vomited and went straight to bed with a terrible headache. By daylight, Gib had died.

Emily remained unwell for months after Gib's death. She remembered watching and applauding from her bedroom window when he had celebrated his birthday just a few months earlier with a procession of drums and horns, marching toward the Homestead and then around the garden beds. Everybody wore cocked hats and the neighbors cheered. She remembered how he rejoiced in secrets. "Dont tell, Aunt Emily!" he would beg her. It was unbearable that he was gone.

She wrote to Sue, "I see him in the Star, and meet his sweet velocity in everything that flies." The doctor diagnosed her with "nervous prostration"—what we today might call a nervous breakdown.

Sue and Austin were broken by their young son's death. Sue would see almost no one, would not even drive through the village for nearly a year. Emily and Vinnie worried especially about Austin. Gib had been his favorite child.

Not until January did Emily start to feel stronger. But she was laid low again in March, with news of Otis Lord's death. She sent a poem to cousins Loo and Fanny that began, "Each that we lose takes part of us." It did indeed seem that with each death of someone dear to her, Emily grew more physically diminished, though her voice was strong in the letters and poems she still wrote. The poems she wrote in the last few years of her life were short and often about death. This one from 1884 could have been addressed to any of the many loved ones she had recently lost:

> So give me back to Death -
> The Death I never feared

Except that it deprived of thee -
And now, by Life deprived,
In my own Grave I breathe
And estimate it's size -
It's size is all that Hell can guess -
And all that Heaven was -

One Saturday in June, Emily and Maggie were baking a cake when darkness overcame Emily. She slipped out of consciousness. Late that night she awoke to find Austin, Vinnie, and an unknown doctor leaning over her, afraid she was dying. She had fainted and remained unconscious for many hours. It was the first time in her life she had had such an experience.

Once alert, she became very sick and stayed in bed for nearly eight weeks, unable to even answer letters. The doctor called it "revenge of the nerves." "But who," Emily was finally able to write to Loo and Fanny, "but Death had wronged them?"

Emily never fully recovered from that illness. She continued to read and write, eagerly awaiting books about one of her favorite writers, George Eliot, and about her dear friend Samuel Bowles. She was enchanted by a popular novel of the times, *Called Back*, which she called "haunting." She was shocked by the unexpected death of Helen Hunt Jackson from stomach cancer in August 1885. She was still sending flowers with her notes to friends that summer, but in November she grew so weak she couldn't leave her room or, often, her bed for long periods of time. Austin was alarmed enough by her symptoms that he canceled a trip to Boston that month. At Christmas she sent her annual note to Kendall Emerson, Gib's friend from the mud hole, as she had done since Gib's death.

Vinnie was often at her bedside during these months, with Austin taking her place for an hour or two when he could. The doctor ordered Emily not to read or write, but she managed to pen occasional letters to Elizabeth Holland, Thomas Higginson, and Loo and Fanny.

On May 13, Vinnie told Austin that Emily was "feeling poorly." He decided not to leave the property that day. Around 10 in the morning, Emily seemed to lapse into unconsciousness. She was breathing heavily. The doctor was called and stayed most of the afternoon. The next day Austin found her much the same. Two neighbors sat with Vinnie. Though he could hardly bear the sound of her labored breathing, Austin waited nearby.

Emily remained unconscious, struggling to breathe, into a third day, May 15. As evening approached, just before 6:00 PM, the awful sound of her breathing stopped. The last words she had written were to Loo and Fanny, just days before she fell into the coma. "Little Cousins," wrote Emily, "Called Back."

The cause of Emily's death has never been clearly established. Her death certificate specifies it as Bright's disease, which is a kidney disorder. A number of factors, however, call this diagnosis into question, and there is no widespread agreement about the cause of her death.

Four days after her death, a simple funeral service was held in the parlor at the Homestead. A minister led the gathered mourners in prayer. Thomas Wentworth Higginson read a poem on immortality by one of Emily's favorite writers, Emily Brontë. Emily, dressed in white, her chestnut-colored hair framing her peaceful face, lay in a white coffin. She was 55 years old but looked decades younger, without a single gray hair or wrinkle. A small bunch of violets, punctuated by one pink flower, lay at her neck. By her hands Vinnie placed two heliotropes, Emily's favorite flower, saying these were "to take to Judge Lord."

Emily had left specific instructions for her burial, and they were followed exactly. The honorary pall-bearers, who included the president and professors of Amherst College, carried the casket out the back door of the Homestead. Then six Irish men who worked on the Dickinson grounds took over, as Emily had desired. With the procession following them, they walked around her flower garden, through the barn, and into the fields of buttercups that led to the West Cemetery, where the Dickinson family plot lay. They lowered her casket into the grave, which Sue had lined with evergreen boughs.

In the obituary that Sue wrote, she mentioned Emily's "seclusion and intellectual brilliance" as "familiar Amherst traditions." She wrote about Emily's poems and her reluctance to publish. But perhaps the truest part of Sue's memorial to Emily were these lines: "So intimate and passionate was her love of Nature, she seemed herself a part of the high March sky, the summer day and birdcall."

With Emily's death were buried the many mysteries of her life. Elusive and enigmatic, she defied understanding in her own lifetime and continues to do so more than a century after her death. The multitude of her poems—as elusive and enigmatic as the poet herself—ask more questions than they answer, which is probably exactly to Emily's liking.

> Because I could not stop for Death -
> He kindly stopped for me -
> The Carriage held but just Ourselves -
> And Immortality.
>
> We slowly drove - He knew no haste
> And I had put away
> My labor and my leisure too,
> For His Civility -
>
> We passed the School, where Children strove
> At Recess - in the Ring -
> We passed the Fields of Gazing Grain -
> We passed the Setting Sun -
>
> Or rather - He passed Us -
> The Dews drew quivering and Chill -
> For only Gossamer, my Gown -
> My Tippet - only Tulle -

We paused before a House that seemed
A Swelling of the Ground -
The Roof was scarcely visible -
The Cornice - in the Ground -

Since then - 'tis Centuries - and yet
Feels shorter than the Day
I first surmised the Horses' Heads
Were toward Eternity -

EPILOGUE

DISCOVERING AND PUBLISHING THE POEMS

Emily's family and close friends were well aware of her commitment to her poetry. They knew that she spent much of her time composing her poems. It was not unusual for one of them to receive a verse enclosed with a letter. So when, after Emily's death, Vinnie took on the task of sorting through her things, she would certainly have expected to find manuscripts written by her sister.

What Vinnie did not expect, however, was to find such an enormous quantity of poems—nearly 1,800, many of them collected and bound by string into small booklets: the fascicles. Countless others were scribbled in Emily's tiny handwriting on scraps of paper or copied in careful writing onto fine stationery. And, of course, there were all the poems Emily included in her letters.

Stunned by the discovery, Vinnie decided that her sister's poems must be published. She asked Sue and

Thomas Higginson, the two people whose opinions Emily had most valued, to go through the enormous collection and select and prepare a group for publication.

Sue believed that Emily's poems should be privately printed and given only to family and close friends. She knew how Emily had felt about publication. Thomas was not prepared to devote himself to such a huge project. Vinnie turned the material over to Sue, but after two years Sue had made little progress. Frustrated, Vinnie asked Mabel Loomis Todd, Austin's lover, if she would take on the work of readying Emily's poems for publication. Vinnie's choice may seem odd, but Mabel was also a writer and, while she had never met Emily, the two had corresponded and appreciated each other's artistic sensibilities. Some scholars point out that were it not for Mabel, the world may never have heard of Emily Dickinson.

Mabel reluctantly agreed, but as she began transcribing and organizing the poems, she grew immersed in the work. She also soon realized that it was too much for one person and persuaded Thomas to share the task.

The two of them tried to edit Emily's unusual poems into forms that would be more accessible to readers. They changed punctuation, played with some of the rhymes, and added titles. In 1890 a Boston publisher issued the first collection of Emily's work, entitled simply: *Poems by Emily Dickinson*. The byline read, "Edited by two of her Friends, Mabel Loomis Todd and T. W. Higginson." Five hundred copies were printed. Two more editions followed, in 1891 and about 1896, also prepared by Mabel and Thomas. The public response to Emily's poems was overwhelming. In 1894, with Vinnie's help, Mabel published a two-volume collection of Emily's letters.

In 1895 Austin died, and the Todds and Dickinsons began to argue over a piece of land that Austin had apparently promised to the Todds in return for Mabel's work on the poems. The argument turned ugly, leading to a lawsuit in 1898. The Todds lost the suit, and in retaliation Mabel locked away the poems and other Dickinson family papers she still had.

But Mabel did not have all the poems, and eventually Emily's niece Mattie, now Martha Dickinson Bianchi, began to prepare a new collection. In 1914, Little, Brown published *The Single Hound: Poems of a Lifetime, with an Introduction by her Niece, Martha Dickinson Bianchi*. Most of the poems in this book were ones that Emily had sent to Sue. Angry, Mabel and her daughter, Millicent Todd Bingham, published an enlarged volume of Emily's letters in response.

The feud between the families resulted in numerous books of Emily's poems and letters published either by Mattie or by Millicent over the following decades. Not until 1955, nearly 70 years after Emily's death, did a complete, three-volume collection of her poetry appear, edited by Thomas H. Johnson and published by Harvard University's Belknap Press. Today scholars continue to research Emily's original scraps, fascicles, and manuscripts for answers to the many questions that still remain about her work and her life.

ACKNOWLEDGMENTS

Writing about the mysterious Emily Dickinson has been a thrilling challenge. I want to thank those who helped this book come into being, starting with my original editor, Lisa Reardon. This was the third book Lisa and I embarked on together, and I am very grateful for her faith in my work and for her perceptive and skillful guidance. My thanks go to Jerome Pohlen for enthusiastically taking over the editorial process from Lisa, and to Ellen Hornor for her thoughtful and thorough attention to the manuscript.

Thank you to everybody at Chicago Review Press for working so hard to make this book so beautiful; special thanks to the talented Giselle Potter for her charming cover illustration. I'm delighted to have her artwork as the face of my book.

I'm grateful to Jane Wald, executive director of the Emily Dickinson Museum in Amherst, Massachusetts, for her guidance in the early days of my research. I also want to express my great appreciation to Dickinson scholar Marta Werner, who vetted my final manuscript, for sharing her expertise and providing thoughtful notes and clarifications. Any errors that remain are entirely my own.

Thanks to all those who helped me obtain the images shown in this book, especially Cynthia Harbeson at the Jones Library in Amherst, Christina Barber at Amherst College, and Leslie Fields at Mount Holyoke, as well as to the helpful staff at the Manuscripts and Archives of Yale University Library and at the Houghton Library of Harvard University.

While I relied heavily on primary sources in writing this book, my research was enormously aided by the esteemed biographers who have come before me. I'm particularly indebted to the work of Alfred Habegger, Richard Sewall, and Cynthia Woolf.

Finally, I want to thank my agent Jennifer Unter for her ongoing support of all of my work.

TIME LINE

1813—Samuel Fowler Dickinson, Emily's grandfather, builds the Homestead

1828—May, Edward Dickinson, Emily's father, weds Emily Norcross

1829—April 16, William Austin Dickinson is born

1830—December 10, Emily Elizabeth Dickinson is born

1833—February 28, Lavinia (Vinnie) Norcross Dickinson is born

1840—Emily's family moves to a house on West (now North Pleasant) Street; Emily begins attending Amherst Academy

1847—September, Emily enters Mount Holyoke Female Seminary

1848—August, Emily leaves Mount Holyoke Female Seminary

1849—Emily's father gives her a brown Newfoundland dog she names Carlo

1852—February, Emily's poem "Sic transit gloria mundi" is published anonymously in the *Springfield Daily Republican* as "A Valentine"—the first known publication of her work

1852—June, Emily's father is elected to the US House of Representatives

1853—June, the railroad comes to Amherst

1855—February, Emily hears the sermons of Charles Wadsworth

1855—November, Emily's family moves back to the Homestead

1856—July, Austin marries Emily's close friend Susan Gilbert

1858—Emily secretly begins creating her fascicles—small booklets of her poems

1861—June 19, Austin and Susan's first child, Edward (Ned) Austin Dickinson, is born

1862—April, Emily begins a lifelong correspondence with Thomas Wentworth Higginson

1864—April, Emily travels to Boston for medical treatment for her eye problems

1865—April, Emily makes a second months-long stay in Boston for eye treatment

1866—February, Emily's poem "The Snake" is published anonymously in the *Springfield Daily Republican*; her dog, Carlo, dies

1866—November 30, Austin and Susan's second child, Martha Gilbert Dickinson, is born

1873—Emily's father is elected to the Massachusetts House of Representatives

1874—June 16, Emily's father dies

1875—August 1, Austin and Susan's third child, Thomas Gilbert (Gib) Dickinson, is born

1878—December, Emily's poem "Success is counted sweetest" appears anonymously in the collection *The Masque of Poets*

Late 1870s—Emily's romance with Otis Phillips Lord begins

1882—November 14, Emily's mother dies

1883—October 5, Gib dies

1884—March 13, Otis Phillips Lord dies

1886—May 15, Emily dies

1890—The first collection of Emily's poetry is published

NOTES

CHAPTER 1: EARLY CHILDHOOD AT THE HOMESTEAD

"the fire": Sewall, *Life of Emily Dickinson*, 323.
"a very good child . . . does not moan": Sewall, 324.
"You must not": Habegger, *My Wars*, 97.
"keep school, & . . . learn, so as to tell me": Habegger, 98.
"My Dear little Children": Sewall, *Life of Emily Dickinson*, 335.
"ramble away with": Emily Dickinson to Susan Gilbert, 11 June 1852, in *The Letters of Emily Dickinson*, ed. Thomas H. Johnson, letter 94. Hereafter, this source will be cited as *Letters*; the number following the title refers to letter number rather than page or volume number.
"things we did when children": Emily to Austin Dickinson, 12 April 1853, in *Letters*, 115.
"frowned with a smile": Emily to unknown recipient, Prose Fragment, 117, n.d.

CHAPTER 2: A BELOVED SCHOOL WITH BELOVED FRIENDS

"very bright, but rather delicate" and *"in both thought"*: Sewall, *Life of Emily Dickinson*, 342.

"the wits of the school": Sewall, 370.

"You cannot think" and *"You must write"*: Emily to Austin, 18 April 1842, in *Letters*, 1.

"he is the silliest" and *"I miss you"*: Emily to Jane Humphrey, 12 May 1842, in *Letters*, 3.

"my thoughts &": Emily to Abiah Root, 28 March 1846, in *Letters*, 11.

"There she lay": Emily to Abiah, 28 March 1846.

"Tell Uncle Wm.": Edward Dickinson to Emily, 7 May 1845, in *Letters*, ed. note to 6.

"the five": Sewall, *Life of Emily Dickinson*, 380.

CHAPTER 3: SCIENCE, NATURE, AND RELIGION

"it seems more like": Emily to Abiah, 23 February 1845, in *Letters*, 5.

"admire the gifts": Sewall, *Life of Emily Dickinson*, 352.

"Most all the girls" through *"I expect I shall"*: Emily to Abiah, 7 May 1845, in *Letters*, 6.

"I never enjoyed": Emily to Abiah, 3 August 1845, in *Letters*, 7.

"I really think" and *"I mean to pick"*: Emily to Abiah, 25 September 1845, in *Letters*, 8.

"back than all": Emily to Abiah, 21 January 1846, in *Letters*, 9.

"I feel that I shall never" and *"How ungrateful"*: Emily to Abiah, 31 January 1846, in *Letters*, 10.

"I think of the perfect happiness": Emily to Abiah, 28 March 1846, in *Letters*, 11.

CHAPTER 4: HIGHER EDUCATION

"I feel that I have not": Emily to Abiah, 8 September 1846, in *Letters*, 13.

"a most witching": Emily to Abiah, autumn 1846, in *Letters*, 15.

"Miss. Lyon & all": Emily to Abiah, 6 November 1847, in *Letters*, 18.

"Home was always": Emily to Austin, 17 February 1848, in *Letters*, 22.

CHAPTER 5: A MERRY LIFE IN AMHERST

"beautiful": Emily to Jane Humphrey, 23 January 1850, in *Letters*, 30.

"the pulses gallop": William Grimes, "She Was No Bird: 'Jane Eyre' Manuscript on First Trip to America," *New York Times*, September 8, 2016, www.nytimes.com/2016/09/09/books/she-was-no-bird-jane-eyre-manuscript-on-first-trip-to-america.html.

"is a year younger": Joseph Lyman to Timothy Lyman, circa 1846–1850, quoted in Sewall, *Life of Emily Dickinson*, 427.

"very very happy": Joseph Lyman to Laura Baker, circa 1856–1858, quoted in Sewall, 137.

"The grave opened": Emily to Jane Humphrey, 23 January 1850, in *Letters*, 30.

"Amherst is alive": Emily to Joel Norcross, 11 January 1850, in *Letters*, 29.

"Life is but a strife": Emily to William Cowper Dickinson, February 1850, in *Letters*, 33.

"Magnum bonum, 'harum": Emily to (possibly) George H. Gould, February 1850, in *Letters*, 34.

"I wish I knew": Henry Shipley, quoted in *Letters*, ed. note to 34.

"Christ is calling": Emily to Jane Humphrey, 3 April 1850, in *Letters*, 35.

"I can't tell you": Emily to Jane, 3 April 1850.

"my kitchen . . .God forbid": Emily to Abiah, 7 and 17 May 1850, in *Letters*, 36.

"I have dared . . . budding, and springing, and singing": Emily to Jane, 3 April 1850.

CHAPTER 6: EMILY AT TWENTY

"is as uneasy": Emily to Austin, 29 June 1851, in *Letters*, 45.

"Did'nt we have": Vinnie, quoted in Emily to Austin, 20 July 1851, in *Letters*, 48.

"boquets fell in": Emily to Austin, 6 July 1851, in *Letters*, 46.

"I arrange my tho'ts": Emily to Austin, 27 July 1851, in *Letters*, 49.

"eternal feelings—how things": Emily to Abiah, 19 August 1851, in *Letters*, 50.

"Home is a holy": Emily to Austin, 25 October 1851, in *Letters*, 59.

"Susie, forgive me": Emily to Susan Gilbert, 11 June 1852, in *Letters*, 94.

"you will find the blue hills": Emily to Austin, 17 October 1851, in *Letters*, 58.

CHAPTER 7: A BUDDING POET

"excessive satisfaction": Emily to Austin, 6 February 1852, in *Letters*, 72.

"Why can't I": Emily to Sue, 11 June 1852, in *Letters*, 94.

"Amherst is growing": Emily to Austin, 20 June 1852, in *Letters*, 95.

"I dont know but it's wrong": Vinnie, quoted in Emily to Sue, late April 1852, in *Letters*, 88.

"she is their's just as much": Emily to Austin, 12 April 1853, in *Letters*, 115.

"I think Father": Emily to Austin, 16 May 1853, in *Letters*, 123.

"thy mother and thy sister": Emily to Sue, 24 February 1853, in *Letters*, 102.

"This is a lonely house": Emily to Austin, 24 March 1853, in *Letters*, 109.

"it will not be as pleasant": Emily to John Graves, February 1853, in *Letters*, 100.

"Write! Comrade, write!": Emily to Sue, March 1853, in *Letters*, 105.

"Now, Brother Pegasus": Emily to Austin, 27 March 1853, in *Letters*, 110.

"Oh Austin . . . Newton": Emily to Austin, 27 March 1853.

"a gentle, yet grave": Emily to Edward Everett Hale, 13 January 1854, in *Letters*, 153.

CHAPTER 8: A SECOND SISTER

"Like some old Roman General": Emily to Austin, June 1853, in *Letters*, 127.

"Sue, you can go or stay": Emily to Sue, late summer 1854, in *Letters*, 173.

CHAPTER 9: BACK TO THE HOMESTEAD

"I'm gayer than": Emily to Sue, 28 February 1855, in *Letters*, 178.
"his congregations were": Sewall, *Life of Emily Dickinson*, 451.
"nervous fever . . . I don't go": Emily to Abiah, 25 July 1854, in *Letters*, 166.
"choose now": Habegger, *My Wars*, 336.
"My only sketch": Emily to Elizabeth Holland, August 1856, in *Letters*, 185.
"I am sorry you came": Emily to Samuel and Mary Bowles, June 1858, in *Letters*, 189.
"I am ill": Emily to Master, about 1858, in *Letters*, 187.

CHAPTER 10: THE POET IN FULL BLOOM

"I can't stay any longer": Emily to Elizabeth Holland, 6 November 1858, in *Letters*, 195.
"I feel the oddest": Emily to Mrs. Joseph Haven, 13 February 1859, in *Letters*, 200.
"Dear cousins": Emily to Frances (Fanny) and Louisa (Loo) Norcross, mid-September 1860, in *Letters*, 225.
"If you will be a good boy": Edward Dickinson to Ned Dickinson, via Sue, 6 December 1861, quoted in Wolff, *Emily Dickinson*, 202.
"cough as big": Emily to Master, about 1861, in *Letters*, 248.
"I hope that ruddy face": Emily to Loo, 31 December 1861, in *Letters*, 245.
"Frazer is killed": Austin, quoted in Emily to Samuel Bowles, March 1862, in *Letters*, 256.
"My friends are": Emily to Samuel Bowles, August 1858, in *Letters*, 193.
"Verse is alive?": Emily to Thomas Wentworth Higginson, 15 April 1862, in *Letters*, 260.

"surgery . . . it was not so": Emily to Thomas, 25 April 1862, in
Letters, 261.

"Tutors . . . a terror": Emily to Thomas, 25 April 1862.

"Could'nt Carlo, and you": Emily to Master, summer 1861, in *Letters*, 233.

"spasmodic . . . uncontrolled": Emily to Thomas, 7 June 1862, in
Letters, 265.

"Let Emily sing for you": Emily to Loo and Fanny, late January
1863, in *Letters*, 278.

CHAPTER 11: SHUNNING SOCIETY, SEEKING SECLUSION

"He is in the habit": Emily to Thomas, early 1866, in *Letters*, 316.

"He inherits his": Emily to Elizabeth Holland, March 1866, in
Letters, 315.

"robbed . . . defeated": Emily to Thomas, early 1866, in *Letters*, 316.

"I do not cross" and *"saved her life"*: Emily to Thomas, June 1869,
in *Letters*, 330.

"If I read": Emily, quoted in Thomas to Mary Channing Higginson, August 1870, in *Letters*, 342a.

"ask[ed] great questions": Emily to Thomas, 26 September 1879,
in *Letters*, 352.

"I find ecstasy": Emily, quoted in Thomas to Mary, August 1870.

"would like it to not end": Edward, quoted in Emily to Thomas,
July 1874, in *Letters*, 418.

"Home is so far": Emily to Thomas, July 1875, in *Letters*, 441.

"I hereby give myself": Edward, quoted in Wolff, *Emily Dickinson*,
126.

"Oh Aunt Emily": Habegger, *My Wars*, 582n.

"You know I": Emily to Ned Dickinson, July 1877, in *Letters*, 511.

CHAPTER 12: THE FINAL YEARS— LOVE, AND MUCH LOSS

"Sweet One . . . Naughty one": Emily to Otis Phillips Lord, about
1878, in *Letters*, 561.

"*most probably*": *Literary World*, 10 December 1878 issue, quoted in *Letters*, ed. note to 573d.

"*closest earthly . . . my 'Heavenly'*": Emily to Charles H. Clark, early June 1883, in *Letters*, 826.

"*The Gentleman with*": Habeggar, *My Wars*, 594.

"*I do—do want you*": Emily to Otis, 30 April 1882, in *Letters*, 750.

"*Did you see . . . He will be*": Dialogue quoted in Emily Otis, 14 May 1882, in *Letters*, 752.

"*The dear Mother*": Emily to Elizabeth Holland, November 1882, in *Letters*, 779.

"*Stay with us*": Emily to Ned, 19 June 1883, in *Letters*, 829.

"*Open the Door*": Gib Dickinson, quoted in Emily to Elizabeth Holland, late 1883, in *Letters*, 873.

"*Please bring me*": "Thomas Gilbert (Gib) Dickinson (1875–1883), nephew," Emily Dickinson Museum website, www.emily dickinsonmuseum.org/gilbert_dickinson.

"*Don't tell, Aunt Emily!*": Gib, quoted in Emily to Sue, early October 1883, in *Letters*, 868.

"*I see him*": Emily to Sue, early October 1883.

"*nervous prostration*": Emily to Elizabeth Holland, late 1883, in *Letters*, 873.

"*revenge of the nerves*" and "*But who*": Emily to Loo and Fanny, early August 1884, in *Letters*, 907.

"*haunting*": Emily to Loo and Fanny, 15 January 1885, in *Letters*, 962.

"*feeling poorly*": Austin, in 1886 diary, quoted in Habeggar, *My Wars*, 626.

"*Little Cousins*": Emily to Loo and Fanny, May 1886, in *Letters*, 1046.

"*to take to Judge Lord*": Thomas Higginson, quoted in Sewall, *Life of Emily Dickinson*, 667.

"*seclusion and intellectual*": Susan Gilbert Dickinson, obituary for Emily Dickinson, *Springfield (MA) Republican*, May 18, 1886, www.emilydickinson.it/edobituary.html.

Bibliography

Dommermuth-Costa, Carol. *Emily Dickinson: Singular Poet*. Minneapolis, MN: Lerner, 1996.

Farr, Judith, with Louise Carter. *The Gardens of Emily Dickinson*. Cambridge, MA: Harvard University Press, 2004.

Franklin, R. W., ed. *The Master Letters*. Amherst, MA: Amherst College Press, 1986.

Franklin, R. W., ed. *The Poems of Emily Dickinson*. Reading Edition. Cambridge, MA: Belknap Press of Harvard University Press, 1999.

Guides at the Dickinson Homestead. *Emily Dickinson: Profile of the Poet as Cook with Selected Recipes*. Amherst, MA: Trustees of Amherst College, 2010.

Habegger, Alfred. *My Wars Are Laid Away in Books: The Life of Emily Dickinson*. New York: Modern Library, 2001.

Johnson, Timothy H., ed. *The Letters of Emily Dickinson*. 3 vols. Cambridge, MA: Belknap Press of Harvard University Press, 1958.

Kelly, Mike, Carolyn Vega, et al. *The Networked Recluse: The Connected World of Emily Dickinson*. Amherst, MA: Amherst College Press, 2017.

Leyda, Jay. *The Years and Hours of Emily Dickinson*. New Haven: Yale University Press, 1960.

Olsen, Victoria. *Emily Dickinson*. American Women of Achievement. Philadelphia: Chelsea House, 1990.

Sewall, Richard B. *The Life of Emily Dickinson*. Cambridge, MA: Harvard University Press, 1980.

Shurr, William H., ed. *New Poems of Emily Dickinson*. Chapel Hill: University of North Carolina Press, 1993.

Werner, Marta, and Jen Bervin. *The Gorgeous Nothings: Emily Dickinson's Envelope Poems*. New York: Christine Burgin/ New Directions, 2013.

Wolff, Cynthia Green. *Emily Dickinson*. Radcliffe Biography Series. Cambridge, MA: Perseus, 1986.

ILLUSTRATED COLLECTIONS OF POETRY BY EMILY DICKINSON

Dozens of collections of Emily's poetry have been published over the years. Below is a selection of illustrated collections meant for a young audience that provide a good introduction to her work.

I'm Nobody! Who Are You? Poems of Emily Dickinson for Young People. Introduction by Richard B. Sewall. Gilsum, NH: Stemmer House, 1994.

Poetry for Kids: Emily Dickinson. Edited by Susan Snively. Lake Forest, CA: Moondance, 2016.

Poetry for Young People: Emily Dickinson. Edited by Francis Schoonmaker Bolin. New York: Sterling, 2014.

Image Credits

Page 39: Mount Holyoke College Archives and Special Collections

Page 52: Todd-Bingham Picture Collection, Manuscripts and Archives, Yale University Library

Page 61: The Emily Dickinson Collection, Amherst College Archives & Special Collections

Page 74: Todd-Bingham Picture Collection, Manuscripts and Archives, Yale University

Page 89: Courtesy of the Jones Library Inc., Amherst, Massachusetts

Page 98: Courtesy of the Jones Library Inc., Amherst, Massachusetts

Page 105: Dickinson Room, Houghton Library, Harvard University

Page 109: Dickinson Room, Houghton Library, Harvard University

Page 120: Dickinson Room, Houghton Library, Harvard University

Page 123: The Emily Dickinson Collection, Amherst College Archives & Special Collections

Page 131: Dickinson Room, Houghton Library, Harvard University

Page 139: Todd-Bingham Picture Collection, Manuscripts and Archives, Yale University

INDEX